The 500 Hidden Secrets of
MIAMI

INTRODUCTION

This book invites you to discover the less-traveled causeways of Miami. The main objective is to point the reader to places that are not usually included in tourist guides, like the rooftop movie theater with a full bar or the hotel with a hidden speakeasy, or to find the places where only locals eat, hang out, and shop. It also lists the most interesting galleries, museums, and other cultural institutions that Miami has to offer. It even includes some unusual experiences, such as swimming in a freshwater Venetian pool, or day trips to the Everglades and the Keys, where visitors can commune with alligators and dolphins.

The guide reflects the fascinating shift that has occurred in Miami in the last decade. South Beach and other parts of Miami Beach made their comeback starting in the early 1990s, and now also Brickell/Downtown and the MiMo District/Upper East Side thrive as neighborhoods in which to live and work. In between, Wynwood, Midtown and Miami Design District have become known as arts, dining and shopping regions. The addresses chosen echo this change, but other parts of sprawling Miami-Dade County have not been neglected.

Finally, this guide cannot possibly mention everything there is to see and do; indeed, there's always something new popping up, and something to mourn that's closed. While continuous reinvention is one of Miami's charms, it also means that this guide can only be a starting point for the discovery of this 'Gateway to the Caribbean'.

HOW TO USE
THIS BOOK?

————————

This guide lists 500 things you need to know about Miami in 100 different categories. Most of these are places to visit, with practical information to help you find your way. Others are bits of information that help you get to know the city and its habitants. The aim of this guide is to inspire, not to cover the city from A to Z.

The places listed in the guide are given an address, including the neighborhood (for example Brickell or Pinecrest), and a number. The neighborhood and number allow you to find the locations on the maps at the beginning of the book: first look for the map of the corresponding neighborhood, then look for the right number. A word of caution however: these maps are not detailed enough to allow you to find specific locations in the city. You can obtain an excellent map from any tourist office or in most hotels. Or the addresses can be located on a smartphone.

Please also bear in mind that cities change all the time. The chef who hits a high note one day may be uninspiring on the day you happen to visit. The hotel ecstatically reviewed in this book might suddenly go downhill under a new manager. The bar listed as one of the 5 places where the rhythm is gonna get you might be empty on the night you visit. This is obviously a highly personal selection. You might not always agree with it. If you want to leave a comment, recommend a bar or reveal your favorite secret place, please visit the website *the500hiddensecrets.com* – you'll also find free tips and the latest news about the series there – or follow *@500hiddensecrets* on Instagram or Facebook and leave a comment.

THE AUTHOR

Jen Karetnick has lived in Miami since 1992, weathering and wondering at its vast changes along the way. A freelance dining critic and food-travel writer, she has covered the city's scintillating food scene since she arrived, prowling from canal to causeway, eating and drinking all the way. As a freelance travel and lifestyle journalist, she also writes for publications including *Southern Living, HuffPost, BobVila.com,* and *Allrecipes.* She is also a poet and author/co-author of 21 books, including four cookbooks. One of those cookbooks, *Mango,* reflects on the two decades she lived on a historic mango grove, where she and her husband raised their two children, rescued various dogs and cats, and farmed 14 mango trees. She now lives with her husband and two miniature dachshunds in another historic home in a designated bird sanctuary, where peacocks freely roam the streets.

The author would like to thank her husband, Jon; their kids, Zoe and Remy; and their friends and neighbors for their recommendations, companionship, and tolerance. She greatly appreciates all the public relations personnel, business owners, restaurateurs, proprietors, chefs, and staffs who provided information and helped coordinate photography. Special thanks to her friends from the GMCVB and Stacy Shugerman and to photographer Valerie Sands for always providing great images that show Miami at its best, in all its outlandishness and awesomeness. Finally, a huge thank you to Dettie Luyten, Katya Doms, and the rest of the Luster team for seeing the enchantment in the Magic City and making the Miami book a firm reality.

DOWNLOAD
TWO FREE WALKS

In addition to selecting 500 hidden secrets in Miami, author Jen Karetnick has also mapped out two city walks. These walks are a great way to explore two of the most culturally relevant and bustling areas in Miami and will also lead you past several of the addresses in the book. The walks are available as digital downloads in the *the500hiddensecrets.com* webshop. As the owner of this book, you get them for free by scanning the QR code below:

MIAMI (NORTH)

overview

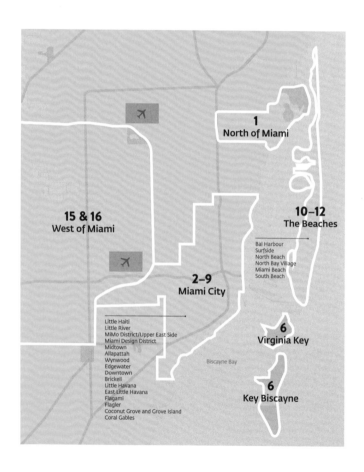

1
North of Miami

15 & 16
West of Miami

10–12
The Beaches

Bal Harbour
Surfside
North Beach
North Bay Village
Miami Beach
South Beach

2–9
Miami City

Little Haiti
Little River
MiMo District/Upper East Side
Miami Design District
Midtown
Allapattah
Wynwood
Edgewater
Downtown
Brickell
Little Havana
East Little Havana
Flagami
Flagler
Coconut Grove and Grove Island
Coral Gables

Biscayne Bay

6
Virginia Key

6
Key Biscayne

MIAMI (SOUTH)

overview

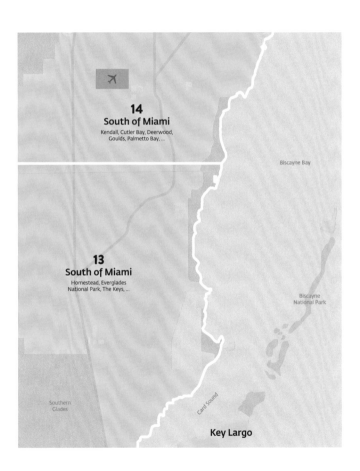

14
South of Miami
Kendall, Cutler Bay, Deerwood,
Goulds, Palmetto Bay, ...

Biscayne Bay

13
South of Miami
Homestead, Everglades
National Park, The Keys, ...

Biscayne
National Park

Southern
Glades

Card Sound

Key Largo

Map 1
NORTH OF MIAMI

MIAMI CITY

OVERVIEW

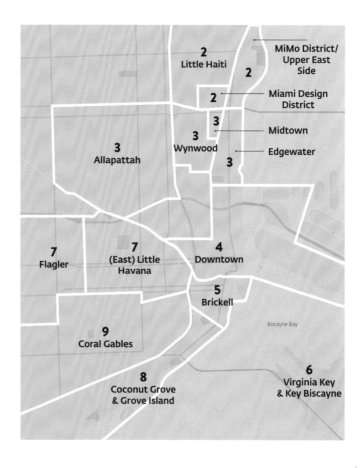

2 Little Haiti

MiMo District/ Upper East Side

2

2 Miami Design District

3 Midtown

3 Wynwood

3 Edgewater

3 Allapattah

3

7 Flagler

7 (East) Little Havana

4 Downtown

5 Brickell

9 Coral Gables

Biscayne Bay

8 Coconut Grove & Grove Island

6 Virginia Key & Key Biscayne

Map 2

MIAMI CITY

LITTLE HAITI, LITTLE RIVER,
MIMO DISTRICT/UPPER EAST SIDE
and MIAMI DESIGN DISTRICT

Map 3

MIAMI CITY

ALLAPATTAH, MIDTOWN, WYNWOOD, EDGEWATER *and* DOWNTOWN

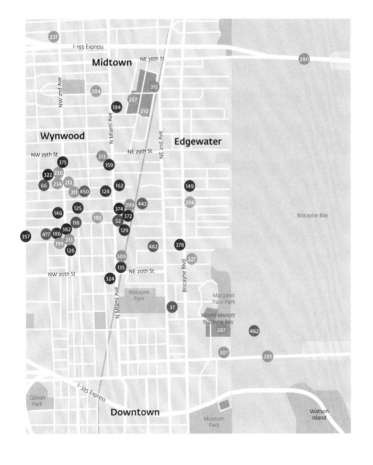

Map 4

MIAMI CITY

DOWNTOWN

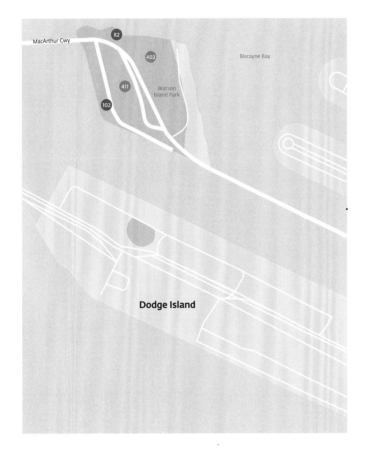

Map 5

MIAMI CITY

BRICKELL

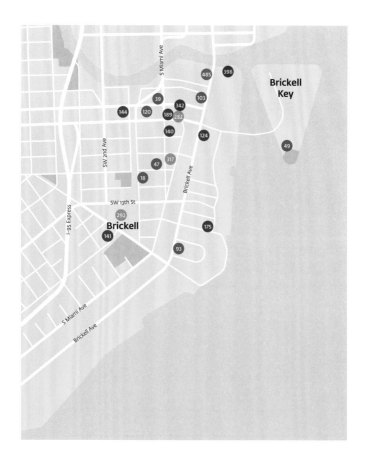

Map 6

MIAMI CITY

VIRGINIA KEY *and* KEY BISCAYNE

Map 7

MIAMI CITY

LITTLE HAVANA, EAST LITTLE HAVANA, FLAGAMI and FLAGLER

347 Overtown

110

LoanDepot
Park

NW 12th Ave

NW 8th Ave

NW 17th Ave

W Flagler St

East Little
Havana

16

SW 1st St

SW 7th Ave

SW 12th Ave

SW 8th Ave

5

365

SW 7th St

255 486

122

SW 8th St

60

68 121 387

361

153 307 339 113

487

308 390

Map 8

MIAMI CITY

COCONUT GROVE *and* GROVE ISLAND

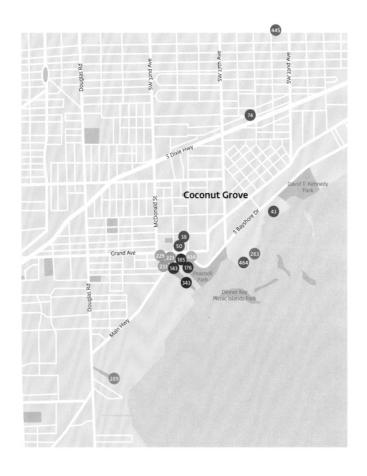

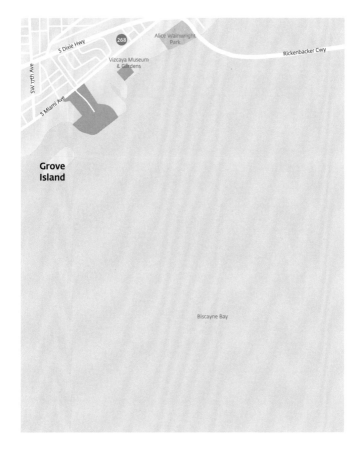

**Grove
Island**

S Dixie Hwy

SW 17th Ave

S Miami Ave

268

Vizcaya Museum
& Gardens

Alice Wainwright
Park

Rickenbacker Cwy

Biscayne Bay

Map 9
MIAMI CITY
CORAL GABLES (NORTH)

CORAL GABLES (SOUTH)

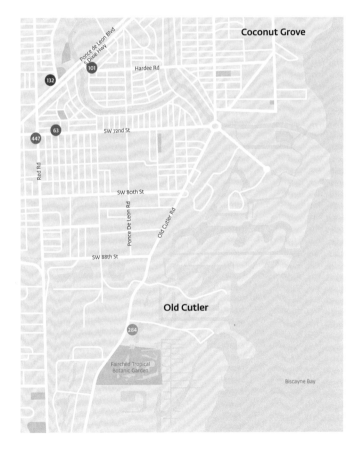

Map 10

THE BEACHES

BAL HARBOUR, SURFSIDE, NORTH BEACH *and* NORTH BAY VILLAGE

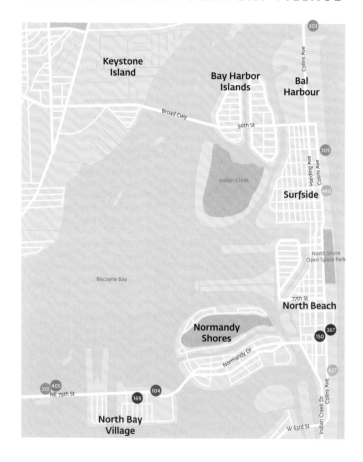

Map 11

THE BEACHES

MIAMI BEACH

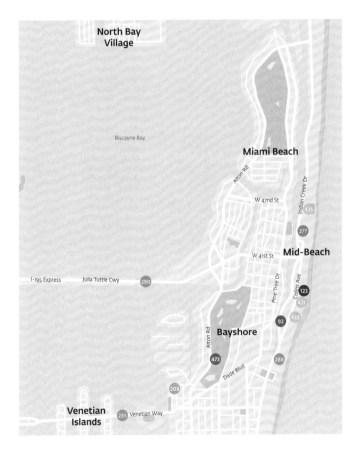

Map 12

THE BEACHES

SOUTH BEACH

Map 13

SOUTH OF MIAMI

HOMESTEAD, EVERGLADES NATIONAL PARK, THE KEYS...

Map 14

SOUTH OF MIAMI

KENDALL, CUTLER BAY, DEERWOOD, GOULDS, PALMETTO BAY, ...

Westchester

Coconut
Grove

SW 40th St

Olympia
Heights

SW 57th Ave

Coral
Gables

Don Shula Expy

SW 88th St

Kendall

S Dixie Hwy

Pinecrest

Palmetto Bay

Biscayne Bay

Cutler Ridge

488
332
40
220
23
30
377
351
164
198
207
235
479
236
35
168
297
13
167
165
41
217

Map 15

WEST OF MIAMI

MIAMI SPRINGS, WEST MIAMI, SWEETWATER, UNIVERSITY PARK, ...

Map 16

WEST OF MIAMI

DORAL and HIALEAH

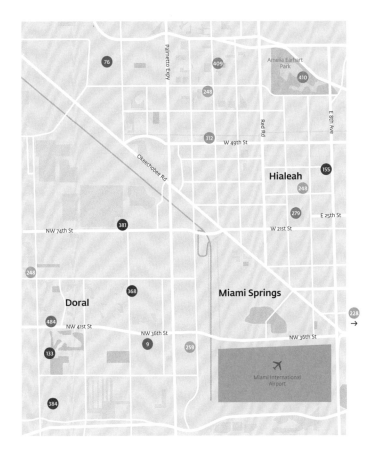

LIGHTKEEPERS

120 PLACES TO EAT OR BUY GOOD FOOD

---

5 great takes on
TACOS and BURRITOS

1 **EL PRIMO RED TACOS**

179 E Flagler St
Downtown ④
+1 502 230 4567
elprimoredtacos.com

Messy and mighty good, these stuffed, pan-fried tortillas that you dip into consommé are totally addictive. But don't neglect the *birria* ramen. A cross between *birria* taco and ramen, it's another item you can't live without once you try it. And then there's the *birria* smash sandwich.

2 **LA SANTA TAQUERIA**

201 NE 82nd St
Little River ②
+1 305 906 1149
lasantataqueria.com

This neighborhood place, with an attached *mezcalería,* is popular for its overstuffed tacos. Go for Taco Tuesday, when most of the items (except for the seafood) come three to an order instead of in pairs. It's difficult to choose between meats – except if you're vegetarian. But don't worry, you're covered too, with mushrooms, quinoa, and cauliflower tacos.

3 **TAQUERÍA LOS NOPALES**

1800 SW 27th Avenue
Shenandoah Park ⑦
+1 786 308 9959
losnopalestaqueria.com

What do you get with a Colombian proprietor and a Mexican chef? Oaxacan soft tacos (try pork rind in green sauce) at their finest. The *birria* – a make-it-yourself stewed dish of moist shreddable pork and white corn served with tortillas, lettuce, radish, and lemon – is also amazing.

4   TACOS VS BURRITOS CANTINA

650 NE 79th St Csy
MiMo District/
Upper East Side ②
+1 305 603 8365
tacosvsburritos.com

It's not a competition, except when it is. Here, they don't *make* you choose, but if you order one of the ginormous burritos, chances are you just won't have room for the soft or fried tacos, as good as they are. Not to even mention any of the other menu items like the *tortas,* Mexican spare ribs, and more.

5   CAJA CALIENTE

808 Ponce De Leon
Boulevard
Coral Gables ⑨
+1 786 431 1947
caja-caliente.com

If you haven't heard of Cuban tacos, take a seat. That is, take a seat in Caja Caliente, where chef Monica 'Mika' Leon welds Mediterranean, Spanish, and Cuban flavors together. Whether you prefer *parga* (fried snapper), *vaca frita* (fried steak), or *lechón asado* (roasted pork) is up to you. Wash it down with Mika's guava lemonade Prosecco spritz.

5 CAJA CALIENTE

5 beloved
C U B A N *restaurants*

---

6 **LITTLE HAVANA RESTAURANT**

12727 Biscayne Blvd North Miami ⓘ
+1 305 899 9069
littlehavana restaurant.com

From ham *croquetas* and *maraquitas* (plantain chips with garlicky mojo) to main courses of *lechón asado* (roasted pork) and *picadillo* (ground beef) with Creole sauce, the classics are all represented at this long-standing favorite. Formally dressed servers are quick to greet families and serve Cuban rolls.

7 **LA CUMBANCHA**

6743 Main St Miami Lakes ⓘ
+1 305 456 5972
lacumbancha miami.com

Suburban sibling to Little Havana's bustling Cafe La Trova, this more expansive spot offers equally as entertaining live Cuban music, delicious cocktails from *cantinero* Julio Cabrera – but a wholly different menu. Start with the rustic bread with olive oil and three salts, then move on to the filet mignon that's flambeed in rum tableside. End with the roasted Manchego cheese flan.

8 ISLAS CANARIAS RESTAURANT

**13695 SW 26th St
Tamiami** ⑮
+1 305 559 6666
*islascanarias
restaurant.com*

Owned and run by the Garcia family since 1977, Islas Canarias is as dependable as thunderstorms in the tropics. Cuban and Spanish dishes include a homemade *tamal,* yellow rice with chicken and sweet plantains, and meatballs Catalan style, served with rice and house-cooked potato chips.

9 KUBA CABANA

AT: CITYPLACE DORAL
**3450 NW 83rd
Avenue, #140
Doral** ⑯
+1 305 800 5822
kubamiami.com

This isn't your *abuela's* Cuban restaurant. Dishes like *yuca-lote (yuca* prepared like Mexican street corn) and *guava pollo barbacoa* (guava-smoked half chicken with spicy guava jus) take the building blocks of Cuban cuisine and jazz them up for modern times. Look for the vintage car out front. A second location is in Bayside.

10 AMELIA'S 1931

**13601 SW 26th St
Tamiami** ⑮
+1 305 554 4949
amelias1931.com

Chef-owner Eileen Andrade named this Parisian bistro-style spot after her grandmother. Located across from her grandfather's Islas Canarias, it combines those classic Cuban flavors with Asian, South American, and French *savoir faire.* The pork belly with homemade sweet chili sauce and fried *queso* and the tongue-tingling *gochujang* paella chock-a-block with shellfish, halibut and peas are only two must-haves.

5 superb
STEAK HOUSES

---

11 EDGE BRASSERIE AND COCKTAIL BAR
AT: FOUR SEASONS
HOTEL MIAMI
1435 Brickell Avenue
Brickell ⑤
+1 (305) 381 3024
fourseasons.com/
miami/dining

With its farm-to-table sourcing and rooftop location – where you're warmed by fire pits when the cool winter weather sets in – the restaurant would never strike you as a corporate entity if you didn't have to go through a hotel lobby to get here. Delicacies include Wagyu churrasco, Australian grass-fed lamb, and Berkshire pork.

12 FIORITO
5555 NE 2nd Avenue
Little Haiti ②
+1 305 754 2899
fioritomiami.com

This charming Argentine spot, run by a trio of brothers, serves a tempting breaded steak Milanesa, topped with ham, tomato sauce and mozzarella. The Rioja-braised short ribs, which arrive with a fried egg (2 dollars extra), rival only the skirt steak with *chimichurri* for your attention.

13 PLATEA PRIME STEAKHOUSE & CEVICHE BAR
12175 S Dixie Hwy
Pinecrest ⑭
+1 305 964 5108
plateamiami.com

The only Peruvian-influenced steakhouse in Miami – and maybe the nation – this place is worth the drive into surburbia if only for its weekly experiences. Who could resist Caymus (wine) Sunday, (filet) Mignon Monday, or Tomahawk Tuesday? Prices are more than fair and quality is stellar.

14 RED SOUTH BEACH

801 South Pointe Dr
South Beach ⑫
+1 305 534 3688
redsobe.com

Chef-partner Peter Vauthy is known for pushing the luxe limits at this South Beach steakhouse. The prime beef cuts are enormous and the free-range veal chops can be ordered as Marsala, Milanesa, Parmigiana or stuffed with foie gras, mushrooms, fontina and truffled Diane. There's even a 4,5-kilogram whole Alaskan king crab available.

15 TORO TORO

AT: INTERCONTINENTAL MIAMI
100 Chopin Plaza
Downtown ④
+1 305 372 4710
torotoromiami.com

Richard Sandoval's pan-Latin steakhouse is a sleeper hit in the lobby of the Intercontinental Hotel. Steaks range from a 12-ounce Wagyu *picanha* to the house special, the Toro Toro tomahawks in a variety of sizes, served with bone marrow butter and *chimichurri*. Don't skimp on inventive sides like grilled avocado with corn *pico de gallo*.

11 EDGE BRASSERIE AND COCKTAIL BAR

5

LATE-NIGHT /
EARLY-MORNING *spots*

---

16 **YAMBO RESTAURANT**
1643 SW 1st St
East Little Havana ⑦
+1 305 649 0203

Hearty and filling Nicaraguan food is
welcome at any time of the day or night,
and so are you at this cheerful place.
Large portions of classic dishes like
grilled steak, pork with *yuca* and *gallo
pinto* (red beans and rice) for almost
ridiculously low prices. Pick up after
clubbing in Little Havana. Open from
10 am till 4:35 am.

17 **LA SANDWICHERIE
MIAMI BEACH**
229 14th St
South Beach ⑫
+1 305 532 8934
lasandwicherie.com

Open daily until 5 am, this iconic
sandwich shop makes French subs that
hit the spot after a night partying in
Wynwood, Brickell, or South Beach (the
last location is the original). Try a Tropical
(avocado, mozzarella, papaya, mango,
pineapple, lettuce and cucumber) or
a SOBE Club (turkey, Brie, and avocado).
Then buy a bottle of the mustard
vinaigrette to take home.

18 MARION MIAMI

1111 SW 1st Avenue
Brickell ⑤
+1 786 717 7512
marionmiami.com

Go for the caviar, stay for the cabaret. This dinner-plus-entertainment place is both delicious and fun, making time go by so fast that your ride-share goes into surge-pricing. Still, it beats a carriage turning into a pumpkin. We also highly recommend booking a table for its signature Thursday Ladies' Night, a soirée like none other in town. Open until late.

19 CHEESE BURGER BABY

1505 Washington
Avenue
South Beach ⑬
+1 305 531 7300
cheeseburgerbaby.net

When you're out partying on South Beach, you know what you need before you (eventually) go to bed: The stomach-filling satisfaction of a fat-driven, carb-backed nosh. Enter the goods at Cheese Burger Baby, open daily until 4 am. The double bacon cheeseburger with a side of onion rings is always a go-to, but you can get any burger or sandwich as a wrap, a bowl, or gluten-free, too.

20 MOSHI MOSHI

7232 Biscayne Blvd
MiMo District/
Upper East Side ②
+1 305 751 2114
moshimoshi.us

Congenial, cozy and open until 5 am daily, this Japanese restaurant offers a range of good eats, from perfectly prepared sushi to noodle soup bowls as big as your head. Try some rarely seen dishes, such as Tako Yaki, octopus 'pancakes' with bonito flakes, and Kimchee Buta, pork sauteed with kimchee.

The 5 hottest
CARIBBEAN
restaurants

---

26 **MANJAY RESTAURANT**
2618 NW 5th Avenue
Wynwood ③
+1 786 542 0990
manjayrestaurant.com

Owned by Haitian-born restaurateur Christian Dominique, Manjay features a range of Caribbean dishes with roots from Haiti to Trinidad to Jamaica. Menu choices include *griyo* (Haitian-style pork), vegan roti, and jerk chicken bites. Whatever you get, accompany it with crispy *banan payzay* and *pikliz* (fried green plantains and a spicy slaw).

27 **CHEF CRÉOLE SEASONAL KITCHEN**
200 NW 54th St
Little Haiti ②
+1 305 754 2223
chefcreole.com

Chef-owner Wilkinson (Ken) Sejour has been called the 'Emeril of Haitian food'. He's especially proficient with zesty fish and seafood; you can tell by both the dishes and his restaurants' oceanic decor themes. Like the marinade, tartar sauce and *pikliz* (spicy vegetable relish)? Buy them to take home or at the online store.

28 B & M MARKET & ROTI SHOP

219 NE 79th St
Little River ②
+1 305 757 2889

Curry goat never tasted as good as it does from this nondescript market, whose door is (literally) almost always open. Not a fan of goat? Not a problem. Guyanese owners Nafeeza and Sheir Ali, also cook up curry shrimp, jerk chicken, stew beef, oxtail and *dhal phourie* (split pea) roti.

29 LORNA'S CARIBBEAN & AMERICAN GRILL

19752 NW 27th Ave
Miami Gardens ①
+1 305 623 9760
lornascaribbean.com

Jamaican-style oxtail. Curry goat. Fried Bahamian *conch*. You'll find a number of Caribbean favorites at this sleek mainstay, which often comes with a side of live music. That's because Ms. Lorna, as everyone calls her, has been making these family recipes for locals since 2006. Which means you should certainly leave room for rum cake.

30 JAMAICA KITCHEN

8736 SW 72nd St
Kendall ⑭
+1 305 596 2585
jamaicakitchen.com

Locals rave about the enormous, price-friendly servings of jerk and curry chicken or pork at this shopping center joint, as well as the Jamaican patties. But don't let that dissuade you from trying the Jamaican-Chinese dishes such as the pork and ham *choy,* a mustard green that lends zingy flavor.

5

FRESH FISH

market-restaurants

---

31 **CAPTAIN JIM'S SEAFOOD MARKET & RESTAURANT**

12950 W Dixie Hwy
North Miami ①
+1 305 892 2812
captainjimsmiami.com

Although Captain Jim's seems to have gotten a bit pricier since being screened on Anthony Bourdain's Parts Unknown, you can usually be assured of a table here. This seafood market and restaurant stocks most of its inventory from its own fleet of boats. No frills, lots of visible chills laid out for viewing on ice.

32 **GARCIA'S SEAFOOD GRILLE & FISH MARKET**

398 NW North
River Drive
Downtown ④
+1 305 375 0765
garciasmiami.com

As Cuban *exilios,* the Garcia family, all fishermen, started their seafood market business in 1966. In the early 1990s, they added this riverside restaurant with outdoor seating and an emphasis on island-style preparations such as conch fritters, ceviche, fish dip, fried, blackened or grilled grouper or *mahi-mahi* fillets.

33 **LA CAMARONERA SEAFOOD JOINT & FISH MARKET**

1952 W Flagler St
Little Havana ⑦
+1 305 642 3322
lacamaronera.com

This joint, stemming from Garcia Brothers Seafood, debuted in 1976 as a Cuban fish fry with stand-up counters. Today the place is still known for its quick service of *pan con minuta,* a fried snapper sandwich. Take-out from the market includes breaded lobster tail and fried grouper cheeks.

34 FRESHCO FISH MARKET & GRILL

12700 SW 122nd Avenue, #113
West Kendall ⑭
+1 305 278 3479
freshcofish.com

This family-owned restaurant opened its Cortland Plaza restaurant in 2018, but they've actually been in the fish biz for more than two decades. That's why the Key West-style menu is so authentic, albeit with a little innovation on the side: You'll find everything from classic conch fritters to ceviche to a Philly shrimp cheese sandwich.

35 CAPTAIN'S TAVERN RESTAURANT

9625 S Dixie Hwy
Pinecrest ⑭
+1 305 666 5979
captainstavern miami.com

Transformed from a post office, this popular restaurant and market has been chugging along since 1971. Important items of note: Along with the fish and seafood selection, some of which come from local indie fishermen, the wine list is stellar. Tuesday is always 2-4-1 Maine lobster night.

35 CAPTAIN'S TAVERN RESTAURANT

5 excellent
OYSTER *bars*

---

36 **SEAWELL FISH N' OYSTER**

AT: KIMPTON ANGLERS HOTEL

660 Washington Ave South Beach ⑬

+1 786 594 5820

seawellmiami.com

A respite from the relentless partylike atmosphere of South Beach, this chill oyster bar and seafood restaurant is a haven for the locals who like the raw stuff on the half shell. Check out the daily selections to slurp down or order them Rockefeller. Either way, count on them being fresh as a slap.

37 MIGNONETTE DOWNTOWN

DAILY : CBGB / CRUDO / WHOLE FISH
WEST   EAST
FANNY BAY   BEAUSOLEIL
ROYAL MIYA⬤   MALPEⓒUE
SUN HOLLOW   PINK MOON

37 MIGNONETTE DOWNTOWN

210 NE 18th St
Edgewater ③
+1 305 374 4635
mignonettemiami.com

Chef-owner Danny Serfer struck gold when he started shucking oysters in this Edge-water spot. The servers know the minute difference between each mollusk. Also available fried or Rockefeller. Lots of daily specials round out the offerings.

38 THE OYSTER BAR
AT: COCOWALK

3015 Grand Avenue
Coconut Grove ⑧
+1 305 603 9009
evacoconutgrove.com

This snug space – only nine bar seats and 20 spots on the terrace – is actually married to another restaurant, Eva. Both are owned by Michael Beltran's Ariete Hospitality Group, so you can count on the crisp quality of the oysters spiked with *pikliz* mignonette. Don't hesitate to try anything more daring as well, such as the clam dip with Peruvian peppers.

39 THE RIVER OYSTER BAR MIAMI

650 S Miami Avenue
Brickell ⑤
+1 305 530 1915
therivermiami.com

The first oyster bar to take root in 2003, courtesy of chef-owner David Bracha, who has had several trend-setting restaurants since the early 1990s. Choose from a half-dozen varieties daily, from Hama Hama to Tatamagouche. Then move on to crudos, ceviches and more fresh fish and seafood, paired with moderately priced wines.

40 THE LAZY OYSTER

4631 SW 75th Avenue
South Miami ⑭
+1 305 907 0257
thelazyoyster.com

Sometimes you just don't want to go out to a restaurant. Maybe it's too beautiful poolside or you're heading out on the boat. Whatever the reason, The Lazy Oyster brings the oyster bar to you via delivery Wednesday-Sunday. Oyster varieties rotate weekly. The Lazy Oyster services places like Gramps Getaway.

The 5 best places to find
S T O N E   C R A B S
without the wait

---

41 GOLDEN RULE SEAFOOD MARKET AND RESTAURANT

17505 S Dixie Hwy
Palmetto Bay ⑭
+1 305 235 0661
goldenruleseafood.com

Opened since 1943 and always in the same location, this intensely local spot has been serving Miami families for generations. Those families know that husband-and-wife team Pam Mullins and Walter Flores will have a trustworthy supply of stone crabs the moment that the season opens until the second it closes.

42 BLUE RUNNER SEAFOOD

11338 Biscayne Blvd
North Miami ①
+1 786 499 9334

Locals know this paneled truck, a family-run business, as the supplier of the freshest fish and seafood, including succulent stone crabs, in the Miami-Dade region. Patriarch Paco Fernando and his team sell them for a lot less than the restaurants do. Caveat: Cracking is do-it-yourself.

43 MONTY'S RAW BAR

2550 S Bayshore Dr
Coconut Grove ⑧
+1 305 856 3992
montysrawbar.com

A happy hour legend, this spot on the bay is best for the views, the live music and stone crabs in season. Modus operandi: Snack on a couple of claws and a few shrimp while watching the sunset and downing a beer after a hot day rather than investing in a full dinner.

44 CJ'S CRAB SHACK

600 Ocean Drive
South Beach ⑫
+1 305 604 5951
cjscrabshack.com

Stone crabs aren't a very well-known menu item here. That could be because it's located on tourist-heavy Ocean Drive. Or because it's in the shadow of a more famous stone crab joint. Or because it's overshadowed by other types of crab. But it is in fact perfect for a quick fix of meaty crab and mustard sauce (along with beach vibes).

45 JOE'S TAKE AWAY

11 Washington Ave
South Beach ⑫
+1 305 673 4611
joesstonecrab.com

Joe's Stone Crab is the restaurant that discovered the edible nature of these sustainable crustaceans, where diners wait hours in line for a table. But at the adjacent Take Away, claws can be packaged to go or consumed in serviceable surroundings, along with the signature accompaniments of hash browns, creamed spinach and key lime pie.

42 BLUE RUNNER SEAFOOD

5 *scintillating*
CEVICHE *sites*

---

46 **PISCO Y NAZCA CEVICHE GASTROBAR**
8405 Mills Dr, #260
Kendall ⑭
+1 305 630 3844
piscoynazca.com

Referencing Peru's famous grape brandy, Pisco y Nazca produces excellent Pisco sours. Pair one with a host of vibrantly flavored ceviches and *tiraditos,* prepared by Executive Chef and native Peruvian Miguel Antonio Gomez Fernández, who was chef de cuisine for celebrity chef Gastón Acurio. Toast such high-end skills at gastropub prices.

46 PISCO Y NAZCA CEVICHE GASTROBAR

47 SUVICHE

49 SW 11th St
Brickell ⑤
+1 305 960 7097
suviche.com

Enjoy this Peruvian specialty reinterpreted. Choose your fresh sea proteins, then your sauce, and have it tossed on the spot. There's also sushi, tartare, tataki, salads and some hot Peruvian fare for those who dislike it raw, plus a Pisco bar at which to soothe a thirst. Additional locations.

48 CVI.CHE 105 DOWNTOWN

105 NE 3rd Avenue
Downtown ④
+1 305 577 3454
ceviche105.com

Founder and native Peruvian Juan Chipoco and partner Luis Hoyos launched this hot spot in 2008, and its ultra-fresh ceviches and *tiraditos* still wow patrons with their authenticity, zing and succulence. The partners have a second site on Lincoln Road.

49 LA MAR BY GASTÓN ACURIO

AT: MANDARIN ORIENTAL, MIAMI
500 Brickell Key Dr
Brickell Key ⑤
+1 305 913 8358
mandarinoriental.com/
miami

This is the first Mandarin Oriental to feature a high-end Peruvian restaurant of renown. While celebrity Peruvian chef Gastón Acurio pops in, the day-to-day is done by Diego Oka, who sculpts fish into attractive, tender cubes and shavings, flavored with South American and Asian influences. Pricey, but worth every dollar.

50 JAGUAR

3067 Grand Avenue
Coconut Grove ⑧
+1 305 444 0216
jaguarrestaurant.com

One of the first Miami restaurants to modernize the way to eat ceviche, this pan-Latin restaurant is a Coconut Grove mainstay. Choose from nearly a dozen beautifully designed ceviches, in several different quantities. The cooked fare is also a gorgeous affair, with influences ranging from Mexico to Brazil.

The 5 most fantastic
FUSION
restaurants

---

51 **FINKA TABLE & TAP**
AT: PLAZA ALEGRE
14690 SW 26th St
Tamiami ⑲
+1 305 227 8818
finkarestaurant.com

Brisket wonton ravioli with cheese sauce. Cuban fried rice, which is a mixture of shrimp, sweet plantains, pineapple, egg, onion and scallion. Owner Eileen Andrade combines Latin and Asian flavors to advantage. As for the tap, try a draft Peruvian or Korean beer, or a craft cocktail garnished with herbs from the restaurant's vertical garden.

52 **OISE RISTORANTE**
AT: OASIS
2335 N Miami Avenue
Wynwood ③
+1 239 980 2912
oisemiami.com

If Italian-Japanese fusion, or *Itameshi,* sounds off-putting to you, then you haven't met Oise chef-owner Brad Kilgore. He makes pesto with *shiso.* He has you dipping *cacio e pepe* breadsticks into peppercorn miso Alfredo or *uni* fondue. His chicken *parm katsu sando,* with *umami pomodoro* and caper kewpie, is perfection.

53 **TASCA DE ESPAÑA**
8770 SW 24th St
Westchester ⑮
+1 305 552 0082
tascadeespana.us

A fascinating duet of Spanish and Indian cuisines. Craving *pulpo a la gallega* (octopus) or chicken tikka masala with garlic naan? Get both! It's also surprising to see a Spanish bakery and a bazaar of Indian accessories, but it works.

54 FUEGO BY MANA

3861 NE 163 St
Aventura ①
+1 786 520 4082
fuegobymana.com

If pickled tongue *barbacoa* wrapped in soft corn tortillas, egg rolls stuffed with pastrami, or *empanadas* that spill pulled brisket tickle your palate, then Fuego has got you covered. This Latin American smokehouse and grill also offers an additional fusion feature that you might find surprising: It's 100 percent kosher.

55 PHUC YEA

7100 Biscayne Blvd
MiMo District/
Upper East Side ②
+1 305 602 3710
phucyea.com

Fo-get *pho* – although you will find an excellent one here, where Cajun influences blend into Vietnamese dishes. This indoor-outdoor spot (sit in the Lantern Garden or one of the interior rooms) succeeds with chef-owner Cesar Zapata's take on summer rolls, *baos,* and a signature noodle dish topped with a soft-boiled egg.

55 **PHUC YEA**

5 awesome
ASIAN *restaurants*

---

56 DUMPLING KING
237 NE 167th St
North Miami Beach ①
+1 305 654 4008
dumplingking
miami.com

Absolutely zero ambiance means you can concentrate on what you came for – Shanghai-style steamed soup dumplings, along with a host of other pan-fried and boiled combinations (string bean and pork; chives, pork and shrimp). Other dishes are all equally tasty and speedily served, which is helpful remembering when there's a wait for a table.

57 BASILIC
VIETNAMESE GRILL
AT: ARENA SHOPS
14734 Biscayne Blvd
North Miami Beach ①
+1 305 944 0577
basilicvietnamese
grill.com

Wonderfully fresh Vietnamese fare, run by a trio of brothers, in a strip mall location. The pho and noodle dishes are always excellent, with huge handfuls of bean sprouts and basil to add in. But don't overlook other dishes from the extensive menu, like the ethereal, pan-fried crepe, and the spicy lemongrass duck.

58 ZAIKA INDIAN CUISINE

2176 NE 123rd St
North Miami ①
+1 786 409 5187
zaikamiami.com

Such consistently and beautifully balanced Indian cuisine from former Taj Mahal Hotel chefs that the owners had to expand to accommodate the demand. Traditional dishes abound, as do Zaika signatures: Malabari Chicken (with coconut curry), Kadale Lamb (with chick peas and roasted spices) and Balchao Shrimp (with vinegar and chilies). Will accommodate special diet requests.

59 BALI CAFE

109 NE 2nd Avenue
Downtown ④
+1 305 358 5751

Indonesian cuisine is hard to come by in Miami, but scarcity doesn't affect quality. Take the singular Bali Cafe, for instance, where you should order the *rijsttafel* – a complete meal with lots of appetizers, entrée and tiny little side dishes – to experience it the first time. And make sure to sample a durian smoothie or purple yam ice cream.

60 LUNG YAI THAI TAPAS

1731 SW 8th St
Little Havana ⑦
+1 786 334 6262
lung-yai-thai-tapas.com

Go to this bona fide dive during off hours, so you can find a seat at the bar top or one of the few outside tables. Then slurp up some awesome spicy glass noodles with seafood and follow it up with a curry. Make sure to order everything from the start. Lingering is not encouraged.

5 awesome
OMAKASE and
PRIX-FIXE MENUS

---

61 **COTE MIAMI**

3900 NE 2nd Avenue
Miami Design
District ②
+1 305 434 4668
cotemiami.com

At this award-winning Korean steakhouse, you can order up a Steak Omakase experience: Japanese Wagyu, American Black Angus, USDA Prime cuts (fresh and dry-aged), and Reserve Cuts (including the A5 Japanese Wagyu). It's all complemented by an array of pickled seasonal vegetables, salads, egg soufflé, two stews with rice and soft serve ice cream topped with soy sauce caramel for dessert.

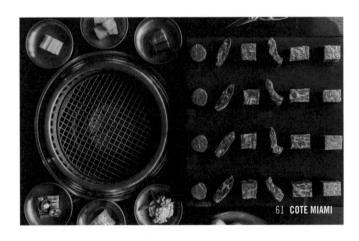

61 COTE MIAMI

62 WABI SABI MIAMI

851 NE 79 St Csy
MiMo District/
Upper East Side ②
+1 305 890 7228
wabisabimiami.com

Miami is replete with high-end *omakase* spots where you can sit for hours and spend thousands of dollars. There's also usually a long waitlist. Wabi Sabi takes care of these potential drawbacks by serving the entire, reasonably priced *omakase* on one plate. No reservation needed. For more formal *omakase,* visit sibling Hiyakawa.

63 FIOLA MIAMI

1500 San Ignacio Ave
Coral Gables ⑨
+1 305 912 2639
fiolamiami.com/
pasta-omakase

This high-end Italian restaurant offers a one-of-a-kind Pasta Omakase. A five-course tasting menu – plus dessert – features the chef's house-made pastas using seasonal ingredients. To that end and in the true fashion of *omakase,* it's chef's choice. But you can find samples of the menu, subject to change, online.

64 LEKU
FISH & GARDEN

AT: RUBELL MUSEUM
1100 NW 23rd St
Allapattah ③
+1 786 464 0615
lekumiami.com

Located within the outstanding Rubell Museum, LEKU features a fantastic LEKU Experience menu filled with Basque cuisine specialties curated by Executive Chef Carlos Garcia. Dishes are inspired by local and seasonal ingredients and many are cooked on the restaurant's outdoor wood-fired Josper grill.

65 CHOTTO MATTE

1664 Lenox Avenue
South Beach ⑫
+1 305 690 0743
chotto-matte.com/
miami

Founded by owner Kurt Zdesar in 2013, this artsy restaurant serves Japanese-Peruvian fare. The combination of flavors is so enticing you'll want to enjoy one of the several 'Nikkei' set menus, which start with vegetarian and go up to include Australian Wagyu grade 8-9.

5

REGIONAL ARTISANS

to sample

---

66 **ZAK THE BAKER**
   295 NW 26th St
   Wynwood ③
   +1 786 294 0876
   zakthebaker.com

Oh, those crusty loaves of Jewish rye sourdough, seeded baguettes and bagels. You can find self-taught, award-winning Zak Stern's unmistakable products at local businesses, or pick them up from his own place. You might as well add in a few pastries while you're at it, or even a whole double chocolate *babka* or cheesecake.

67 **MIMMO'S MOZZARELLA ITALIAN MARKET, CAFÉ & CHEESE FACTORY**
   475 NE 123rd St
   North Miami ①
   +1 305 351 6826

Owner Bruno Ponce has a gold mine of mozzarella here, and it's an endless vein – you go in for one cheese and come out with five different types, including burrata, smoked, stuffed, even a Gorgonzola made from mozzarella. The cafe offers paninis and salads, too.

68 **AZUCAR ICE CREAM COMPANY**
   1503 SW 8th St
   Little Havana ⑦
   +1 305 381 0369
   azucaricecream.com

The line at this Cuban creamery is always long. That's because the ice-cream flavors reflect the neighborhood's culture as well as the owner's heritage. For some, a scoop of the trademarked Abuela Maria, with jellied guava, cream cheese and Maria cookies, is frozen nostalgia. For others, it's novelty. For all, it's a treat.

69 PROPER SAUSAGES

9722 NE 2nd Avenue
Miami Shores ①
+1 786 334 5734
propersausages.com

Proper means done right. And these sausages are exactly that, made with prime cuts and flavored with first-rate, regional ingredients. That's how you wind up with sausages such as The Wynwood Porter and The Lamb & Rosemary. Owners Danielle and Freddy Kaufmann also cook lunch to go; supply restaurants; run an online shop; and deliver.

70 ARTPIE

6732 NE 4th Avenue
Little River ②
+1 305 469 2362
artpieusa.com

A pastry chef by training, founder Monique Font Delacroix first created these 28-plus varieties of savory and sweet handheld pies in her Key Biscayne restaurant. Today she focuses solely on these treats, all named after famous women, making them with vegan dough, organic meats, cheeses, and vegetables, and a whole lotta love.

67 MIMMO'S MOZZARELLA ITALIAN MARKET

The 5 best places for
PASTRIES

---

71 CAFÉ CRÈME

750 NE 125th St
North Miami ①
+1 786 409 3961
cafecrememiami.com

French pastries can make anyone give up on diet. Here, the luscious house-baked *éclairs* – try the coffee flavor for a little Miami influence – are rivaled by the hard-to-find Paris-Brest and a distinct strawberry Napoleon. Even if your waist can't, at only 4,95 dollars each, you can afford more than one. A second location is in Upper Buena Vista.

72 MAX'D OUT ARTISINAL DONUTS

14871 Biscayne Blvd
North Miami Beach ①
+1 305 705 3425
maxdoutdonuts.com

Award-winning pastry chef Max Santiago was the first to bring wacky, weird, and wonderful donuts to Miami. Here, he presents 52 unusual flavors, some available year-round and some rotating monthly. *Café con leche* and *guava con queso* are signature favorites, and for those on special diets, the PB&J and chocolate and peanut butter are vegan and gluten-free.

73 KARLA BAKERY

6474 W Flagler St
West Miami ⑮
+1 305 267 9000
karlabakery.com

Pastelitos. Utter it and amazing, flaky puff pastries filled with sweet guava, mamey or apple will fall into your hands – all for less than one dollar each. Karla also makes *empanadas, croquetas, churros,* rice pudding or custard cups and *yemitas,* as well as Cuban breads and cakes. Multiple locations.

74 THE ORIGINAL DAILY BREAD MARKETPLACE

2400 SW 27 St
Coconut Grove ⑧
+1 305 856 0363
dailybread
marketplace.com

A good *baklava* is not easy to find in Miami, let alone an entire bakery counter. But this all-in-one Middle Eastern marketplace has a plethora of pleasures, including bird's nests, *burma* pastries (pistachio or cashew), fragrant *namoura* and date-or nut-filled *mamoul* cookies. And, of course, outstanding walnut or pistachio *baklava.*

75 TRUE LOAF BAKERY

1894 Bay Road
South Beach ⑫
+1 786 894 6602
trueloafbakery.
square.site

If you've been looking for a bakery that can make a classic Venezuelan *pan de jamón* as expertly as it can a French *kouign amann,* well, you've found it. And just when you've discovered the rustic olive bread you like best, the bakery comes out with another loaf of something. Carb lovers, meet your Mecca.

5
LATIN SPECIALTIES
to try before leaving Miami

---

76 **FRITA**
AT: CUBAN GUYS,
VILLAVERDE
SHOPPING CENTER
**3174 W 76th St
Hialeah** ⑯
+1 786 507 4494
*cubanguys
restaurants.com*

The *frita* is a burger where the beef is mixed with chorizo, then fried, topped with skinny potato fries and onions, and served on a Cuban roll. Sometimes you'll see packaged potato sticks and no onions. Which is why you want to try it at Cuban Guys, who are specialists. Multiple locations.

77 **TEQUEÑOS**
AT: CHARLOTTE BAKERY
**1499 Washington Ave
South Beach** ⑫
+1 305 535 0095

This long-running bakery offers a mix of Latin and European specialties. So anything made with dough here is spot on, including the *tequeños,* which are mildly salty *queso blanco* (white cheese) logs covered with pastry and deep-fried. Be careful when you bite into them – they can squirt like lemons.

78 PÃO DE QUEIJO
AT: BOTECO
916 NE 79th St
MiMo District/
Upper East Side ②
+1 305 757 7735
botecomiami.com

Pão de queijo is a Brazilian cheese roll with an elastic quality to it. It's made with cassava, so it's gluten-free, and filled with mild white cheese similar to mozzarella. At Boteco, a spot-on Brazilian restaurant with live music, karaoke nights and futbol always on the television, it's the first item on the menu.

79 EMPANADAS
AT: HALFMOON
EMPANADAS
860 NE 79th St
MiMo District/
Upper East Side ②
+1 305 532 5277
halfmoon
empanadas.com

This commissary caters and supplies restaurants, but it also has a walk-up window and an exterior counter with stools. Snack on any of the savory pastries filled with ham and cheese, spinach, beef or chicken – plus signature combos like pulled pork with guava barbecue sauce – while you wait for a dozen to be packed up.

80 AREPAS
AT: DOGGI'S AREPA BAR
7281 Biscayne Blvd
MiMo District/
Upper East Side ②
+1 786 558 9538
eatdoggis.com

Like pita bread made with cornmeal, these *arepas* are filled with a variety of stuffings, ranging from chicken salad to fried eggs with avocado. The restaurant is also known for its *cachapas* (corn pancakes) with cheese inside as well as *patacons,* sandwiches made with fried plantains instead of bread. Great for the gluten-intolerant. A few locations.

The 5 most wonderful
WATERFRONT
restaurants

---

81 **BLACK POINT OCEAN GRILL**
AT: BLACK POINT MARINA
24775 SW 87th Ave
Homestead ⑬
+1 305 258 3918
blackpoint
oceangrill.com

There's nothing like snacking on smoked fish dip and peel-n-eat shrimp after a long day of boating, fishing or other water sports. This marina restaurant welcomes all come-as-you-are customers, and it'll also cook your catch as long as you've cleaned it, and give you two sides to boot for 12,99 dollars per person.

82 **JOIA BEACH**
AT: JUNGLE ISLAND
1111 Parrot
Jungle Trail
Watson Island ④
+1 305 400 7280
joiabeachmiami.com

If you want to put your toes in the sand, you can. That's because this restaurant is located on a literal beach. Go for bottomless brunch. Go for *aperitivos* and happy hour, made all the better for watching the waves. Go for dinner and dance the night away. Just make reservations – and don't wear stilettos.

83 **SEA GRILL RESTAURANT**
3913 NE 163rd St
North Miami Beach ①
+1 305 945 7555
seagrillmiami.com

Don your most expensive labels to dine at this lovely Greek restaurant on the Intracoastal. Then order grilled calamari stuffed with feta cheese or jumbo shrimp infused with lemon and oregano. Just be careful to not squirt it on the neighbor's 50.000-dollar Birkin.

84 **IL GABBIANO**
335 S Biscayne Blvd
Downtown ④
+1 305 373 0063
ilgabbianomia.com

This white-tablecloth Italian restaurant, a mainstay in Miami, has impeccable fare, with fish flown in daily and pastas cooked tableside. The view is equally as memorable, given that it's located in a high-rise overlooking Biscayne Bay. Sit on the patio and watch the boats speed toward the horizon while you dine.

85 **SEASPICE BRASSERIE & LOUNGE**
412 NW North River Drive
Downtown ④
+1 305 440 4200
seaspice.com

Seaspice has been a celebrity hangout since it launched, with the requisite photos on its website to prove it. But what's not as well-known is just how gorgeous it is to sit outside on the banks of the Miami River – even during the summer months – and watch the yachts dock while you sup on bouillabaisse and grilled whole *branzino*.

82 JOIA BEACH

The 5 best spots for
SANDWICHES
and BURGERS

---

86 **KABOBJI**
3055 NE 163rd St
North Miami Beach ①
+1 305 354 8484
eatkabobji.com

If a sandwich is only as good as its bread, then Kabobji is the best around thanks to its house-made pita, which is constantly flying out of the oven. Stuffed with lamb kabob, chicken shawarma, or falafel – to name a few options – and topped with homemade tahini or garlic sauce, these wraps are wonderfully satisfying.

87 **CHICK'N JONES**
1601 Drexel Avenue
South Beach ⑫
+1 305 335 0538
chicknjones.com

Jones-ing for an excellent fried chicken *sammie?* With lettuce, pickled veggies, Muenster cheese, and 'love sauce,' this super crunchy one takes care of just about any craving. As does the hot honey version with Southern slaw. Chef-owner Amaris Jones takes good, punny advantage of her last name to make sure you know you'll be satiated here.

88 ROYAL CASTLE

2700 NW 79th St
Little River ②
+1 305 696 8241
royal-castle.
business.site

Once a chain with more than 175 locations, this quick-service burger joint is down to a singular unit in a neighborhood that is safer during the day but also rapidly gentrifying. It's known for small sliders, topped with grilled onions and a pickle. Inexpensive.

89 TINTA Y CAFÉ

1315 Ponce de Leon
Boulevard
Coral Gables ⑨
+1 305 285 0101
tintaycafe.co

Every regular who frequents this place has a favorite pressed Cuban-style sandwich, be it the Croqueton *(croqueta,* ham, mortadella, swiss, pork, mustard, pickles), the Jardinera (veggies with goat cheese and garlic aioli and olive spread) or the house special Tinta y Café (pork, prosciutto, manchego cheese, roasted red peppers, caramelized onions). You'll soon have one, too.

90 MOTEK

19565 Biscayne
Boulevard, #938
Aventura ①
+1 786 953 7689
motekcafe.com

Miami is having a Middle Eastern moment and Motek, with several locations, is all over the city for it. You should be too, especially for the double short rib burger, topped with *arugula,* caramelized onions, and pomegranate-mint aioli. Or the *arayes* burger, a Lebanese grilled beef-stuffed pita served with *tahini* and pickles. The crispy schnitzel sandwich is also a winner.

5

RESTAURANTS
that are SO MIAMI

---

91 **LA CAÑITA**
AT: BAYSIDE MARKETPLACE,
2ND FLOOR
401 Biscayne Blvd
Downtown ④
+1 305 392 0811
lacanitamiami.com

Miamians love James Beard Award-winning chef Michelle Bernstein and partner/husband David Martinez. This Caribbean-Latin American concept, hiding in plain sight at Bayside Marketplace, offers terrific waterfront views, live music curated throughout the week, and a menu that ranges from smoked wahoo fish dip to braised oxtail to vegan *picadillo*. It is so very Miami!

92 **27 RESTAURANT**
& BAR
AT: FREEHAND MIAMI
2727 Indian Creek Dr
Miami Beach ⑪
+1 786 476 7020
27restaurantmiami.com

Located in a historic house, this restaurant screams local. And the menu as well as the decor reflects that philosophy, with items like Florida middleneck clams, Florida fish dip, and local daily catch vying for attention. Produce is grown right outside and influences from the owners' native South America and Middle East also play into the fare.

93 DOCE PROVISIONS

541 SW 12th Avenue
Little Havana ⑦
+1 786 452 0161
doceprovisions.com

Chef-owners Justin Sherrer and Lisetty Llampalla use local products, marry them to various Latin influences, and emerge with some truly creative dishes. They include goat cheese croquettes with guava marmalade; *lechón asado* buns with *aji amarillo* and pineapple confit; and fried chicken with sweet plantain, waffle, pickled peppers and *sriracha* honey. It's both homey and hip.

94 MANDOLIN AEGEAN BISTRO

4312 NE 2nd Avenue
Miami Design
District ②
+1 305 749 9140
mandolinmiami.com

In 2009, husband-and-wife team Ahmet Erkaya and Anastasia Koutsioukis reconditioned a house to fashion this mostly outdoor Greek-Turkish restaurant. You can't help but be seduced by the dips and salads, kebabs, moussaka and whole grilled fish as you dine under the large shade trees that have been there since the 1940s.

95 LA FRESA FRANCESCA

59 W 3th St
Hialeah ①
+1 786 717 6886

This strip-mall bistro is run by a French-Cuban husband-and-wife team, Benoit Rablat and Sandy Sanchez. It's a beautiful marriage, as is the *pastelito de foie gras and guyaba* – seared Hudson Valley Foie Gras in pastry, topped with local guava and toasted pistachios. This is also one of the only places in Miami you can order rabbit (and you should).

The 5 best restaurants for
SPECIAL DIETS

---

96 VEGAN CUBAN CUISINE

9640 SW 72nd St
Kendall ⑭
+1 786 292 0564
vegancubancuisine.com

The name says it all. Miami's first vegan Cuban restaurant makes all the classics – Imperial rice, Cuban sandwich, *croquetas* – only it creates them with plant-based materials. What a win for the vegan community, a large part of which is Cuban, given the culture here! Pick up, have it delivered, or dine outside while the interior is being constructed.

97 MILK GONE NUTS

18829 Biscayne Blvd
Aventura ①
+1 786 654 2973
milkgonenuts.com

Long before everyone was drinking oat, almond and other nut milks, owner Sara Tacher was making shakes, smoothies and other treats from plant-derived liquids in a pop-up spot in a gas station. Fast forward from 2013 and now, in addition to her namesake products, you can also get great juices, ice pops, wraps and *açai* and *pitaya* bowls at her flagship location in Aventura.

98 OSTROW BRASSERIE & O'S RAW BAR

4850 NW 2nd Avenue
Buena Vista ②
+1 786 238 7452
ostrowbrasserie.com

Chef-owner Olivia Ostrow's Brasserie and O's Raw Bar, presented by her collaborator, Michelin-starred chef Michael Collantes is all completely kosher, from the duck confit and signature dish lamb *paupiette* to the 'seafood' tower served at Sunday brunch, filled with creative fish dishes and caviar. The Art Nouveau-designed restaurant also features 40 art pieces from Ostrow's own collection.

99 PLANT THEORY CREATIVE CUISINE

AT: THE LINCOLN EATERY
723 N Lincoln Lane, #112
South Beach ⑫
+1 786 872 1901
thelincolneatery.com/plant-theory

This vegan, gluten-free and keto spot in the heart of South Beach is all about the healing of earth and human. Other buzzwords that will float your kombucha boat? Non-GMO, seasonal and organic. Go-to items include raw and cooked foods such as the Southern Baked Artichik'n sandwich, the Guava Mariahhh BBQ sandwich, the Viva La Quesadilla, and the Neatball Sub.

100 ITTLE LITALY

3808 SW 8th St
Coral Gables ⑨
+1 305 444 3826
ittlelitaly.com

With an Italian twist, this cafe features menu items like marinated mushrooms stuffed with cashew cheese and garnished with pesto, bruschetta on toasted sprouted grain bread, pizzas served both warm and cold, and raw lasagna and zucchini pasta dishes. Mostly but not all raw.

The 5 best bottomless
BRUNCHES

---

101 MAMEY
AT: THESIS HOTEL MIAMI
1350 S Dixie Hwy
Coral Gables ⑨
+1 305 266 2639
mameymiami.com

Chef Nicolas Mazier takes inspiration here from global islands, ranging from the Caribbean to French Polynesia. That's noticeable in touches like the guava jam that accents the Croq Mamey and the poke bowl with mango. Most importantly, though, is the bottomless mimosa option, offered with your choice of orange, pineapple, or grapefruit juice, as well as peach purée.

102 THE DECK AT ISLAND GARDENS
888 MacArthur Cwy
Watson Island ④
+1 786 627 4949
islandgardens.com/
the-deck

This stunning waterside restaurant and lounge is located in the only private superyacht marina in North America, which is complete with a helipad. It's great for a night of Ibiza-like partying or Capri-like happy hour snacking. It's also wonderful for a two-hour bottomless brunch on a day when the water sparkles as much as the bottomless Taittinger Brut does.

103 HUTONG

600 Brickell Avenue
Brickell ⑤
+1 786 388 0805
hutong-miami.com

If you like your brunch spicy, this one's for you. Hutong offers a bottomless Sunday Bubbles and Bao Brunch that includes some pretty zesty Northern Chinese dishes. In tune with the trends, the restaurant also features a 'dark brunch' on Saturday nights with live entertainment such as fire eating. Add on The Flaming Peking Duck for more fun with fire. Now that's hot!

104 SHUCKERS WATERFRONT BAR & GRILL

1819 79th St Cwy
North Bay Village ⑩
+1 305 866 1570
bestwesternon
thebay.com/shuckers-
waterfront-grill

Despite the video on the website, Shuckers is much more of a locals' place than a boat party paradise (although you can pull up your water ride for dockside service at any time). Landlubbers also love to come here on weekends for bottomless bloody Mary brunches along with steak and eggs or vanilla-rum French toast.

105 TANUKI

1080 Alton Road
South Beach ⑫
+1 305 615 1055
tanukimiami.com

When you feel like day-drinking Bloody Marys with bottomless pan-Asian appetizers and *maki* – as well as a choice of entrée and chef's selection of dessert for the table – head to Tanuki. And if you decide that's not enough, you can add on a la carte dim sum and Peking duck. Rest assured, you definitely won't need dinner. Saturday and Sunday.

5 locals' favorites for
PIZZA

---

106 EVIO'S PIZZA & GRILL

12600 Biscayne Blvd
North Miami ①
+1 305 899 7699
eviospizza.com

Even with a roster of specialty pizzas – try The Gyro, with gyro meat, Roma tomatoes, onions and tzatziki sauce – it's the basic New York-style cheese pizza that has folks raving about Evio's. A slice folds just right in your hands.

107 'O MUNACIELLO

6425 Biscayne Blvd
MiMo District/
Upper East Side ②
+1 786 907 4000
munaciello-miami.com

Modeled after its big sibling in Florence, this colorful establishment produces pizzas under Pizza Master Carmine Candito. His experience and heritage shows in each crisp pie – including the black pizzas that incorporate edible charcoal – that emerges from the brick oven, custom-made in Naples.

108 LA NATURAL

7289 NW 2nd Avenue
Little River ②
+1 305 419 0377
lanaturalmiami.com

The chewy-crisp sourdough pizzas with blistered crusts, created by co-owner Javier Ramirez, are just one of the draws here. The natural wines, curated by the other co-owner Andreina Matos, are another. The small plates, created by chef Diego Moya, make a third reason to check out this Little River eatery, an almost entirely outdoor locale that gives good vibes.

109 HARRY'S PIZZERIA

1680 Meridian Ave
South Beach ⑫
+1 786 991 9511
harryspizzeria.com

Launched in 2011 by James Beard Award-winning chef Michael Schwartz and named for his son, this gourmet pizza mini-chain was the first of its kind in Miami. Varieties range from classic margherita to quirky, with toppings like slow-roasted short rib, Gruyère, caramelized onion, and arugula, or spinach *crema,* fontina, and artichoke.

110 CRUST

68 NW 5th St
Downtown ④⑦
+1 305 371 7065
crust-usa.com

This renovated house by the Miami River has become known for Mediterranean dishes of all kinds. But the pizza is what many diners return for, especially when craving specialties like Honey-Truffle Pizza with blue cheese, walnuts, arugula, honey, and white truffle oil. Toppings abound, and gluten-free crust is available.

107 'O MUNACIELLO

The 5 best
TROPICAL FRUIT
markets

---

111 EL PALACIO DE LOS JUGOS

5721 W Flagler St
Flagami ⑮
+1 305 264 8662
elpalaciodelosjugos.com

If it's in season, you'll find it at this incredible market, which stocks every kind of tropical fruit imaginable. Have them juiced or blended as a smoothie. You can also have a delicious Cuban meal. Time in Miami is not complete without a stop here. Nearly ten iconic locations.

112 ROBERT IS HERE

19200 SW 344 St
Homestead ⑬
+1 305 246 1592
robertishere.com

This fruit stand in Homestead's mango and avocado groves has become a stop on the tourist trail. Don't let that deter you. On your way to Everglades National Park, it's an ideal pit stop for a milkshake, some ultra-fresh produce and preserves, and an awesome Instagram image posing with the vintage farm vehicles parked out front.

113 LOS PINAREÑOS FRUTERIA

1334 SW 8th St
Little Havana ⑦
+1 305 285 1135

This small, family-run, open-air market makes fresh juices and smoothies while you wait. Plenty of coconuts await to be lopped off with a machete and handed to you with a straw. There's also fresh sugarcane, bananas, melons, mangos, avocados and citrus.

114 LA JUGUERA TROPICAL

10140 SW 56th St
Olympia Heights ⑮
+1 305 595 3488

An all-in-one grocery store, *ventanita* and cafeteria allows you to shop, take out *café Cubano* and sandwiches, and even have a full meal. The produce is a lovely assortment of everything you need to eat, juice and cook with in a tropical household: citrus, bananas, sugarcane, avocado and more.

115 SOUTHWEST COMMUNITY FARMERS' MARKET

AT: TROPICAL PARK
7900 SW 40th St
Olympia Heights ⑮
+1 305 663 0917
swcommunity farmersmarket.org

While much of the South Florida produce is harvested from November to May, the picking season for tropical fruits is the opposite. That's why this market is open year-round on Saturdays from 9 am to 3 pm. Stop by Farmer Fred of the Redland and Benny's Produce in particular for seasonal fruits like mangos and avocados, carambola, jackfruit and bananas.

112 ROBERT IS HERE

5 *fantastic*
FOOD HALLS

---

116 THE LINCOLN EATERY
   723 N Lincoln Lane
   South Beach ⑫
   thelincolneatery.com

A couple of things make this food hall stand out from the others: 1) It's designed by Arquitectonica, who put the Miami architecture scene back on the map during the 1980s, and 2) The global vendors, which range from Thai to French to Mexican *paletas,* include three kosher concepts. The wide appeal sells.

117 ALTON FOOD HALL
   955 Alton Road
   South Beach ⑫
   altoneats.com

This food hall blends into a neighborhood, and that's what you'll find inside: Neighbors getting lunch to go, grabbing a bite for dinner, or joining friends for a drink at the center bar, Airmail. And while it seems small at first glance, it's actually packed with food options ranging from tacos to Korean food bowls to Mediterranean sandwiches.

118 1-800-LUCKY

43 NW 23rd St
Wynwood ③
+1 305 768 9826
1800lucky.com

The funkiest and hippest of the food halls
– as befitting its artsy locale – 1-800-LUCKY
was also one of the first. It remains one
of the favorites for its all-Asian concept.
You can get everything here from sushi
to dim sum to bubble tea, and even get
in some karaoke time with friends.

119 JULIA & HENRY'S

200 E Flagler St
Downtown ④
+1 786 703 2126
juliaandhenrys.com

Named for two of the historic characters
responsible for founding Miami, this
food hall is a revamp of the five-floor Art
Deco Walgreen's building. It's a combo
of restaurant and music, so you can grab
food from numerous vendors and watch
live performances. Or hang out in the
hipster basement music bar, participate
in holiday celebrations, or play in weekly
game nights.

120 CASA TUA CUCINA

AT: BRICKELL CITY CENTRE
70 SW 7th St
Brickell ⑤
+1 305 755 0320
brickellcitycentre.com/
whats-here/directory/
casa-tua-cucina

This high-end, attractive space includes
everything you could want. Whether you're
looking for fresh or imported ingredients
to bring home or a meal to have on the
spot, Casa Tua Cucina, designed by the
same team behind the famed Casa Tua
Restaurant on South Beach, has your best
Italian interests at heart.

WYNWOOD BREWING COMPANY

70 PLACES
FOR A DRINK

5 places where
THE RHYTHM IS GONNA GET YOU

---

121 BALL & CHAIN

1513 SW 8th St
Little Havana ⑦
+1 305 643 7820
ballandchain
miami.com

Hugely popular on Calle Ocho, especially on weekends, this historic bar was established in 1935 as a saloon, then as a nightclub featuring live jazz. Today it's a mainstay that books acts ranging from Grammy-nominated headliners to salsa bands to DJs. Always colorful, always representative of Miami culture. No cover but often a wait; 21+ after 8 pm.

122 CAFÉ LA TROVA

971 SW 8th St
Little Havana ⑦
+1 786 615 4379
cafelatrova.com

Trova music was created by roving musicians in Cuba. In Café La Trova, they move around from stage to bar, with bartenders whipping out extra instruments to join in. Patrons dance not just on the dance floor but all over. With mixologist Julio Cabrera in charge of cocktails, you'll be hard-pressed to roam elsewhere.

123 THE LIVING ROOM

AT: FAENA HOTEL
MIAMI BEACH
**3201 Collins Avenue
Miami Beach** ⑪
+1 305 534 8800
*faena.com/miami-
beach/dining/
the-living-room*

Get a sense for Miami's local music scene by taking a seat in this cosmopolitan living room. Live music nightly includes bands with original songs to DJs spinning vinyl every Tuesday. Accompany the beats with eggs from Caviar Russe and a stellar selection of cocktails. Reservations strongly suggested.

124 KOMODO LOUNGE

**801 Brickell Avenue
Brickell** ⑤
+1 305 534 2211
komodomiami.com

This pan-Asian restaurant is a steady forerunner (make reservations to dine). But for music, take your Golden Geisha, Samurai Jack and Pikachu cocktails upstairs on the third floor, where owner and nightlife aficionado David Grutman books live musicians and DJs on the weekends. The names are always a surprise, but expect celebrities.

125 GRAMPS

**176 NW 24th St
Wynwood** ③
gramps.com

A favorite with the locals, Gramps features a different genre, from indie punk bands to DJs to R&B, nightly. It also features drag shows, game nights, and arts events. And to be clear, there's a warning to those who imbibe too many Gramps Old Fashioneds: Tip automatically applied to tabs left open overnight.

5 great COCKTAIL
and BEER GARDENS

126 ASTRA

2121 NW 2nd Avenue
Wynwood ③
+1 786 602 3449
astramiami.com

It's easy to feel like you're in Spain or Greece at the lush top of this Wynwood building, where bougainvilleas climb the walls, comfy couches dot the scene, and you can see the sun set from 360 degrees. But the offerings at this beautiful outdoor cocktail garden (and restaurant) will always remind you that you're in Miami.

127 BIKINI HOSTEL CAFE & BEER GARDEN

1255 West Avenue
South Beach ⑫
+1 305 253 9000
bikinihostel.com

An inexpensive, international gathering place. Traveling students who stay in the hostel, and even those who don't, order buckets of beer to drink in the courtyard after a day on the beach or a night on the town. The food is also cheap and always available, from breakfast all day to late-night after-club bites.

128 VEZA SUR BREWING CO.

55 NW 25th St
Wynwood ④
+1 786 362 6300
vezasur.com

When you've gotta have Taco Tuesday but you're also thirsty as heck, head to this Mexican-inspired beer garden. With outdoor seating, giant games, live music and mezcal on Wednesday nights, and plenty of beer (and beer cocktails) on tap, it's just like a German Biergarten. But it has that quintessential tropical touch the accent – and sunshine – that is pure Miami.

129 HIGHER GROUND

AT: ARLO WYNWOOD
**2217 NW
Miami Court**
Wynwood ③
+1 786 522 6600
*higherground
wynwood.com*

Located on the third floor of the Arlo Hotel, Higher Ground is a hidden tropical forest – and a mighty refreshing one at that. Access it from inside or via a brightly painted staircase from street level. Then delight in an outstanding craft cocktail program that's complemented by chef Brad Kilgore's small, rotating menu of raw plates and seafood dishes.

130 CUCKOO CLOCK BRAUHAUS

99 NW 54th St
Little Haiti ②
+1 786 963 0149
cuckooclockmiami.com

If you pine for the Alpines, head to the Cuckoo Clock, where the design, fare, drink, and even live music is determinedly Germanic. In fact, if it weren't for the warm weather and the tropical plants, you might truly believe you're enjoying an après-ski brewski in this Bavarian *biergarten*.

The 5 best
BREWPUBS and
GASTROPUBS

131 **BULLA GASTROBAR**
2500 Ponce De Leon
Boulevard
Coral Gables ⑨
+1 305 441 0107
bullagastrobar.com

In Miami, brewpubs come in all ethnicities. Here you can get your futbol on, choose from an extensive beverage list, and nosh on both traditional and creative tapas like Iberian ham croquettes with fig jelly or the signature *huevos Bulla* (eggs, homemade chips, Serrano ham, potato foam and truffle oil). A second location in Doral.

132 **TITANIC BREWERY & RESTAURANT**
5813 Ponce De Leon
Boulevard
Coral Gables ⑨
+1 305 667 2537
titanicbrewery.com

The closest off-campus bar to University of Miami also happens to be the first, award-winning brewpub in Miami's history. Owner Kevin Rusk developed the concept in 1995, which was a nod to the cruise industry, not the movie. Try the local *mahi-mahi* or peel-and-eat shrimp with a Triple Screw while listening to live blues jams.

133 MIA BRUHAUS

10400 NW 33rd St,
#150
Doral ⑯
+1 786 801 1721
miabruhaus.com

Outpacing Wynwood, Doral is set to become the city's brewing center. The Bruhaus means business, too, with 54 draft lines – 12 offered year-round, the others periodically – and a wide-ranging menu. Fill up on ham *croquetas, tequeños,* and pulled pork *tostones* that have Miami's signature all over them.

134 OFF SITE

NANO BREWERY
+ KITCHEN
8250 NE 2nd Avenue
Little River ②
offsite.miami

You'll never find more than the Super Good Lager and another beer or two to choose from here. But rest assured that the selection is always outstanding, as is the fare. The Burger, Country Cuban and Reuben Sandwich are all reliably delicious. Still, watch the Instagram: You never know when a lobster roll session or a collab with another creator is about to take place.

135 KUSH WYNWOOD

2003 N Miami Avenue
Wynwood ③
+1 305 576 4500
kushhospitality.com/
locations/kush-
wynwood

With local sourcing from just about every craft beer, farm and food artisan in the region, owner Matthew Kuscher has made this tiny Wynwood storefront a hotspot. Go here for the Homestead guacamole, the Kush-branded burgers, the Proper Sausages served with fried pickles, the Florida Gator Tacos and of course an extensive list of craft brewskis.

5 lo-fi
LISTENING LOUNGES

---

136 DANTE'S HI-FI+
519 NW 26th St
Wynwood ③
danteshifi.com

The first vinyl listening lounge in Wynwood, Dante's hit on the audiophile trend and stayed there. Resident music director Rich Medina plays from his own extensive collection. A reservation gets you 1,5 hours to listen to it with cocktail in hand in a vibe-y, living room-like setting filled with other lo-fi fans.

137 MANGROVE
AT: JRK!
103 NW 1st Avenue
Downtown ④
+1 786 734 0834
mangrove.miami

Located behind Jrk! Jamaican restaurant, Mangrove is a listening lounge with a retro look and vintage barware that matches its red, red wine beats. And if you get hungry from too many Pass the Dutchie cocktails, you can always order some hot patties or jerk skewers to take the edge off.

138 MIAMI SOUND BAR
123 SE 2nd Avenue
Downtown ④
+1 786 809 0900
miamisound.bar

Miami Sound bar is an entry into the downtown low-tech ambient scene being embraced by generations X-Z. Modeled after Hi-Fi bars in Tokyo, this place offers a carefully curated vinyl listening experience that's matched only by its sense of humor with its cocktail program, which offers such beauties as the One Hit Wonder.

139 JOLENE SOUND ROOM

200 E Flagler St
Downtown ④
jolenesoundroom.com

You might have guessed by the name what female superstar inspired this place. But Dolly Parton isn't the only female voice you'll hear here. This snug spot, located in the basement of the Julia & Henry's food hall, is an ode to the 1970s, when women began to dominate the airwaves via disco, folk, and more.

140 THE LISTENING BAR

AT: KAORI
871 S Miami Avenue
Brickell ⑤
+1 786 878 4493
kaorimiami.com/
listening-bar

Given that listening bars developed in Japan, it seems only right that this cocktail bar for audiophiles is in an Asian restaurant. When Miami's dancing-on-the-tabletops scene gets to be too much, retire to this acoustically designed lounge, where listening to Hi-Fi is about as high as the action gets.

136 DANTE'S HI-FI+

5 romantic
ROOFTOP VENUES

---

141 VISTA ROOFTOP BAR
AT: NOVOTEL
MIAMI BRICKELL
1500 SW 1st Avenue
Brickell ⑤
+1 786 600 2600
novotelmiami.com/
food-drinks

At this sky-high pool bar, enjoy everything from movie nights with a screen perched over the infinity edge pool to daily happy hour to Saturday Sunset Sessions, which start with sunbathing and end in moonglow. This rooftop pool bar has it all, including a DJ, tapas, drink specials, and stunning views of the Brickell skyline.

142 SERENA AND
THE UPSIDE
AT: MOXY MIAMI
SOUTH BEACH
915 Washington Ave
South Beach ⑫
+1 305 600 4292
marriott.com

The Moxy actually has two enticing rooftops to hopscotch between. Have a drink or dinner on the lower level at Mexican restaurant Serena. Then wander up onto The Upside, that features a pool, daybeds and lounge spaces, and bar. Enjoy happy hour or an aperitif featuring 360 degrees of South Beach.

143 LEVEL 6
3480 Main Hwy –
6th Floor
Coconut Grove ⑧
+1 786 800 2080
level6miami.com

This delightful Spanish concept offers unparalleled views of Biscayne Bay and the surrounding greenery of Coconut Grove. Relax into comfy armchairs, share a few tapas, sip some cocktails, and watch the sun go down over the water. For heartier appetites, try the paella with cava.

144 ROSA SKY

AT: AC & ELEMENT HOTEL
MIAMI DOWNTOWN
**115 SW 8th St,
22nd Floor
Brickell** ⑤
+1 786 745 7486
rosaskyrooftop.com

Think pink. Literally. Not only is Rosa Sky's decor neon Barbiecore, its wine list is filled with fine rosés. And cocktails like the Rosé Mule and Violet Vixen are berry inspirational. This beanstalk of a lounge, one of the more recent and most decorative to grow into the giant Brickell skyline, has direct access from a street-facing elevator.

145 ROOFTOP CINEMA CLUB SOUTH BEACH

**1212 Lincoln Road
South Beach** ⑫
*rooftopcinemaclub.
com/Miami*

Is this a rooftop outdoor movie theater with a bar, or a rooftop outdoor bar with a movie theater? You decide. Just know that you're welcome to arrive early and enjoy all that the venue has to offer, which includes a full menu, full bar, and plenty of golden hour light for shooting pictures of yourself toasting the sunset.

144 ROSA SKY

5 cool
COFFEE SPOTS

---

146 **PANTHER COFFEE**
2390 NW 2nd Avenue
Wynwood ③
+1 305 677 3952
panthercoffee.com

Miami's first independent coffee mini-chain has been a rousing success. It roasts its own coffee in small batches, not only supplying itself but restaurants and cafes. In its own locations, it also serves baked goods and wine, and fosters appreciation of the arts, both visual and performing. A true Miami institution.

147 **NEVERLAND COFFEE BAR**
17830 W Dixie Hwy
North Miami Beach ①
+1 786 916 3560
neverlandcoffeebar.com

This charming throwback – vaguely Peter Pan-themed – is a welcome place to work, meet friends, or simply sit alone and smell the literal flowers in the garden. An extensive menu is served all day. But don't neglect the beverages, especially the hot golden coffee, made with espresso, almond/coconut milk, turmeric, cinnamon, coconut oil, ghee, brown sugar and condensed milk.

148 VICE CITY BEAN

AT: THE CITADEL FOOD HALL
8300 NE 2nd Avenue
Little River ②
vicecitybean.com

Whenever a Miamian says they work from home, they really mean they work from Vice, drinking everything from a mocha with Camino Verde Ecuadorian chocolate to a Luz Helena Salazar Colombian nitro cold brew to a *cajeta* latte inspired by Mexico. And eating overnight oats and cinnamon rolls, too, while they're at it.

149 MAGDALENA COFFEE BAR & HOUSEPLANTS

321 NE 26 St
Edgewater ③
magdalenacoffee.com

In a sea of Miami neon, this eclectic Latin American coffee bar is a tiny, natural, emerald gem. The décor is green-and-white, every nook is stuffed with a plant, and the handcrafted coffees and pastries are outstanding. There's even merch for those who want to advertise this secret spot, although it's small enough to make you think twice.

150 CACHITO COFFEE AND BAKERY

251 71st St
North Beach ⑩
+1 786 973 8614
cachitocoffee.com

This appealing Latin-American coffee shop displays its heart on the surface of your cappuccino or latte. Designs change depending on which artisanal barrista is on duty, as do the daily, house-made *empanadas,* croissants, quiches, pies and tarts. Check the chalkboard for what's available, but do check in. Prices beat national chains, and so does atmosphere.

5 classic

VENTANITAS

(walk-up windows)

---

151 THREE PALMS CUBAN CAFÉ

11500 Biscayne Blvd
North Miami ①
+1 305 891 0046
threepalms
restaurant.com

Named for both a small Cuban town and the three employees that the owner started with, Three Palms always has a crowd. Locals still recall when the Kardashians stopped by this authentic *cafecito*.

152 VERSAILLES

3555 SW 8th St
Little Havana ⑦
+1 305 444 0240
versailles
restaurant.com

Brush up on Cuban coffee vocab before you saunter up. You'll need to know the difference between a *cafecito* (with sugar) or a *cortadito* (with sugar and steamed milk). Then open your ears along with your lips. You'll hear the most incredible political and celebrity gossip – though hardly any of it's true.

153 EL PUB RESTAURANT

1548 SW 8th St
Little Havana ⑦
+1 305 642 9942
elpubrestaurant.com

This long-running Cuban diner has made it into movies like *War Dogs* and become hip again. It becomes crowded at mealtimes, 3.05 pm (Miami's official coffee break!), and around midnight, after partiers on Calle Ocho want to sober up with a *colada*, a *cafecito* meant to be served like booze in shots.

154 SANGUICH DE MIAMI

2057 SW 8th St
Little Havana ⑦
+1 305 539 0969
sanguich.com

The organic meat is roasted on the premises, the bread is homemade, and even the pickles and condiments come fermented straight from the kitchen instead of jars. That's how Cuban sandwiches were made by Cuban grandmothers, and that's how they're made at this joint, run by husband-wife team Rosa Romero and Daniel Figueredo. Order them to go with *batidos*.

155 MOLINA'S RANCH RESTAURANT

4090 E 8th Avenue
Hialeah ⑯
+1 305 693 4440
molinasranch
restaurant.com

Here's the equation for a successful Cuban restaurant: family run + traditional recipes = dedicated patrons. Molina's is all that plus close to Miami International Airport; thus politicians and celebrities make it a first stop. Keep one eye on the *café Cubano,* the other on the clientele.

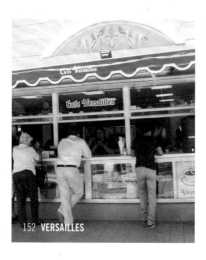

152 VERSAILLES

The 5 best
COCKTAIL
throwbacks

---

156 **EL SALÓN**
AT: ESMÉ HOTEL
1438 Washington Ave
South Beach ⑫
www.esmehotel.com/
drinking-dining/
el-salon

Not only does the fringe-y décor give off vintage flamenco-meets-speakeasy airs, but the drinks do, too. The cocktail menu has sections for retro and tiki quaffs as well as an entire list devoted to martinis. The house also makes its own liquor blends, which all feels very 1960s and delightfully James Bond-ish.

157 **BAR NANCY**

157 BAR NANCY

2007 SW 8th St
Little Havana ⑦
+1 305 397 8971
nancy305.com

Named after a Colonial ship, the
Revolutionary War-themed bar Nancy
is run by renowned mixologists and
features live music programming. Try the
secret, off-menu drink, the 'VIP Captain's
Call' (30 dollars): your favorite base spirits
and flavor profiles custom crafted and
served in a take-home octopus glass.

158 TAPAS Y TINTOS

448 Española Way
South Beach ⑫
+1 305 538 8272
tapasytintos.com

In business since 1982, this bar is a study
in Spanish relics, with vintage costumes
from matadors to futbol players to
flamenco dancers decorating the walls.
It's also a retrogressive homage to gin,
with 18 different brands available.

159 SPANGLISH RESTAURANT & COCKTAIL BAR

2808 N Miami Avenue
Wynwood ③
+1 786 870 4258
spanglishmiami.com

This craft cocktail bar, with its Cafetera
Old-Fashioned and Vice Sour and Dolce
& Banana, gets points for puns, nostalgia,
and noticing what Miamians all sound
like, no matter what their nationality or
ethnicity. It also gets decor cred with those
tufted banquettes and a mural that makes
us think of South Beach in the fifties.

160 FLOYD MIAMI

AT: CLUB SPACE
34 NE 11th St
Downtown ④
+1 786 618 9447
floydmiami.com

Located within the uber-popular Club
Space, Floyd is a separate room where you
can find musical artists, craft cocktails,
and a distinctly speakeasy vibe. Dedicated
to late nights and locals, Floyd hosts indie
album drops, live band sets, DJ residencies
in support of homegrown festivals,
pioneering producers – and liquor promos.

5 takes on
TEA and SYMPATHY

---

161 SPECIALTEA LOUNGE & CAFÉ
AT: COLUMBIA
SHOPPING PLAZA
10766 SW 24th St
University Park ⑮
+1 305 554 8327
specialtealounge.com

This lounge was the first eco-friendly tearoom in Miami. Today it continues to raise the level of earth consciousness as it serves more than 60 varieties of loose leaf teas, *bobas* and frozen teas, as well as natural, homemade sandwiches and desserts. Stay as long as you like. Free Wi-Fi.

162 BUBBA TEA N SMOOTHIES
2617 N Miami Avenue
Wynwood ③
+1 786 391 0851
bubbateamiami.com

A play on the word *boba*, Bubba Tea offers Taiwanese bubble tea, made with fruit-flavored, jellied, or tapioca pearls. For the milk teas, flavors range from chocolate to matcha to Vietnamese coffee. Fruit teas include passionfruit, lychee, and winter melon. And the *boba* also have a variety of flavors. Smoothies are also available.

163 MIU'S TEA

1520 Washington Ave
South Beach ⑫
+1 786 216 7028
miustea.com

A great selection of expertly brewed tea, milk tea, iced tea lattes, fresh fruit tea, and sea salt crema teas are available at this zen little shop. Choose from black, roasted or golden *oolong,* Ceylon, *tieguanyin,* matcha, jasmine, and more to drink on the beach or in the tea garden at their second location in South Miami.

164 THE ENCHANTED DOLLHOUSE

7212 SW 57th Avenue
South Miami ⑭
+1 305 662 2966
theenchanted
dollhouse.com

Visit here for all the pastel florals and French frills that your heart desires. This Parisian-influenced tea room offers an elaborate afternoon tea service with *madeleines* or *macarons* (choose between four menus), along with other goodies. You can also take tea workshops and hold events like children's birthday parties and showers.

165 MY TEA BAR

AT: THE FALLS
8888 SW 136th St
Kendall ⑭
+1 786 732 7078
myteabar.net

Owner Mariedna Castro began her business as a pop-up. It soon progressed to its current brick-and-mortar status, serving its seasonal, anti-oxidant, loose-leaf teas to whoever wants or needs them. The minimalistic, pretty aesthetic is just as soothing as the tea itself, and a perfect place to practice mindfulness and explore creativity.

5

OLD-TIME DIVES

---

166 MAC'S CLUB DEUCE

222 14th St
South Beach ⑫
+1 305 531 6200
macsclubdeuce.com

Owned and run by Mac Klein from 1964 until his death at 101 in 2016, Miami's oldest bar has received a lot of attention since its earlier days. Still, you'll find no muddled cocktails or craft beer. Open 8 am to 5 am seven days a week, with 2-4-1 happy hour from 8 am to 5 pm.

167 CORBETT'S SPORTS BAR & GRILL

12721 S Dixie Hwy
Kendall ⑭
+1 305 238 0823
corbettssportsbar
miami.com

When you're in the mood for darts and 50 cent 'special grilled' wings, or a few bottles of beer and watching the basketball game on one of the 18 televisions, this is the place. Cheap drink specials and events like Ladies Night, Live Trivia and Karaoke. Lots of regulars, who tend to gawk at strangers.

168 KEG SOUTH

10417 S Dixie Hwy
Pinecrest ⑭
+1 305 284 9296
kegsouthpinecrest.com

Open since the 1960s, this institution is famous for its burgers, its wings and, of course, its beer, as the name suggests. A very casual hangout for families, college students and sports fans. Not grimy, but good and dive-y.

169 HAPPY'S STORK LOUNGE & LIQUOR STORE

1624 79th Street Cswy
North Bay Village ⑲
+1 305 865 3621
happysmiami.com

A mixture of native hipsters and old-timers frequent this lounge, which you could easily dismiss if you didn't know better. Great for basic drinks, domestic beers, a game on the television and cheerful drunks. Eat before you come unless you can subsist on nuts, chips and booze. Open from 11.30 am until 5 am.

170 TED'S HIDEAWAY

124 2nd St
South Beach ⑫
+1 305 532 9869
tedshideaway.net

One of the few remaining places in South Beach where you don't have to pretend to be something you're not. Grab a few drinks and watch the game with friends or by yourself. Don't dress or wear cosmetics. Don't even shower. No one here cares. Open noon to 5 am daily.

166 MAC'S CLUB DEUCE

5 joints for
DRINKING LIKE
A LOCAL

---

171 THE ANDERSON

709 NE 79th St
MiMo District/
Upper East Side ②
+1 305 757 3368
theandersonmiami.com

Run by locals for locals, The Anderson is deceptive. It looks fairly nondescript from the road, but inside it's part tiki bar, part piano bar, and part shake-it-til-you-forget-how-old-you-are bar. This is where residents come before and after hurricanes, to celebrate victories large and small, and to beat back the work-week blues.

172 ABBEY BREWING CO.

1115 16th St
South Beach ⑬
+1 305 538 8110
abbeybrewinginc.com

If you're into The Grateful Dead, craft beer – and not much else – Abbey Brewing Co. is your place. Brewmaster Raymond Rigazio opened here in 1995; the locals who weren't models and celebs gave thanks; and the brewpub's history and future were written simultaneously. Open 1 pm to 5 am every day.

173 LOST BOY DRY GOODS

157 E Flagler St
Downtown ④
+1 305 372 7303
lostboydrygoods.com

Contrived to be unpretentious – yes, that's a contradiction, but so is Miami – Lost Boy is where the Gen Z and Millennial crowd from Brickell go to drink rebooted classic cocktails and order from a small but nicely composed menu. The slogan here is 'straightforward/no nonsense' and that's largely what you get, albeit with clients who wear designer clothing.

174 MAMA TRIED

207 NE 1st St
Downtown ④
mamatriedmia.com

If Mama tried to keep us away from this bar, she failed. That's because locals can't resist this place, decorated like an episode of The Brady Bunch. The cocktails are trendy without being outlandish; the beer list is craft-y and local-ish; and there's a decent collection of wines by the glass, including some bubbly. Cash only.

175 LPM RESTAURANT & BAR

1300 Brickell Bay Dr
Brickell ⑤
+1 305 403 9133
lpmrestaurants.com/ miami

Known as La Petite Maison to the uninitiated, LPM is the bar in favor for the well-heeled Gen X and Boomer crowd that lives nearby. The long bar offers enough room to dine should you choose. And the mixologists are masters of their craft who often come up with inventive and artistic drinks to keep regulars coming back.

The 5 best
WINE BARS

---

176 GLASS AND VINE

2820 McFarlane Rd
Coconut Grove ⑧
+1 305 200 5268
glassandvine.com

Under Miami native chef Giorgio Rapicavoli's direction, the menu here reflects the city's culture and regional farms, while the select wine list is sourced from all over to match such innovative dishes as pork 'steak frites' with charred scallion, fried *yuca* and *mojo* butter.

177 NIU WINE

134 NE 2nd Avenue
Downtown ④
+1 786 542 7070
niukitchen.com/
niu-wine

Sited next to the renowned NIU Kitchen, which serves Catalan cuisine, NIU Wine concentrates on natural *vino*. Pair these oft-funky sips with small bites of seafood such as razor clams with sherry vinegar, marinated sardines with grated tomato, or mussels *escabeche* courtesy of Barcelonian chef Deme Lomas. Reservations: yes.

178 VINYA

328 Crandon Blvd,
#122-123
Key Biscayne ⑥
+1 305 361 7007
vinyawine.com

A wine market plus a bistro is just what this island ordered. No need to go to the mainland when you can visit chef Mariano Araya's well-stocked selection of Latin American and European vintages to drink with a wide assortment of fare that covers the same global ground. A second location is in Coral Gables.

179 MARGOT NATURAL WINE & APERITIVO BAR

AT: INGRAHAM BUILDING
21 SE 2nd Avenue
Downtown ④
+1 786 431 5355
margotnatural
winebar.com

Located in a historic building, with a natural stone floor and wood stools to match, Margot is the cool girl on the block. The natural wines rotate, but if you like what you drink, you can also buy to take home. And a spare but thoughtful menu – sardine *bahn mi,* anyone? – is curated to complement. From the team behind Broken Shaker.

180 HIDDEN BODEGA

7613 Biscayne Blvd
MiMo District/
Upper East Side ②
+1 787 246 7770
hiddenbodega
miami.com

From Sunday-Wednesday, this wine shop closes at 5 pm. But on Thursday, Friday, and Saturday, it turns into a secret social scene. Choose a bottle of *vino* (or beer, hard seltzer, or hard lemonade) from the market and head out on the terrace for sips, sunsets, and tapas, and enjoy until midnight.

176 GLASS AND VINE

5 irresistible

JUICE BARS

---

181 MIAMI SQUEEZE

18315 W Dixie Hwy
North Miami Beach ①
+1 305 935 9544
miamisqueeze.com

Open since the mid-90s, Miami Squeeze put juice bars as well as vegetarian and vegan fare on the map in this city. Among the first to serve green juices, cleansing mixes, and juice shots, it also sweetens smoothies with honey. In the mood for something even colder? Try the frozen mango lemonade. And stay for breakfast or lunch.

182 GUARAPO JUICE BAR & CAFÉ

553 NE 81st St
MiMo District/
Upper East Side ②
+1 786 452 1622
guarapomiami.com

A multitude of cleanses, juice blends, smoothies and supplements are available to drink here. There's also a whole list of drinks for what ails you. Acne? Try the pineapple/carrot/apple. Hangover? Tomato/ginger/lemon/cane juice. From helping high blood pressure to easing your ulcers, Guarapo has got you covered. And for solids, there's quinoa bowls, sandwiches and wraps.

183 UNDER THE MANGO TREE

737 5th St
South Beach ⑫
+1 786 558 5103
mangotreemiami.com

This tiny shop is a powerhouse player in the juice world. That's because the product, as well as the intention, is pure. Owner Patricia Olesen has created some irresistible combinations, ranging from the 'Pink Dragon' with dragon fruit, banana and apple to hot and cold healthy teas and coffees like the 'Superfood Frap'.

184 DEVIA JUICE BAR

AT: THE SHOPS
AT MIDTOWN MIAMI
3401 N Miami Avenue
Midtown ③
deviajuicebar.com

Run by the Devia siblings and based on preventative medicine, this juice bar gives you what you need most: vitamins and minerals the way nature intended, through your food. Try freshly blended juices, ginger shots, smoothies made with almond or coconut milk, and *chia, pitaya* and *açaí* bowls. Add superfoods like *spirulina,* hemp seeds, and *moringa.* You'll walk out feeling better than you did walking in.

185 JUICENSE

2992 McFarlane Rd
Coconut Grove ⑧
+1 786 409 2371
juicense.com

Created by specialists from New York, the juices here have up to five pounds of fresh fruit and vegetables pressed into each bottle. Whether you're looking to detox, cleanse, boost the immune system or simply enjoy some fresh vitamins and minerals, the liquids here – including nut milks and smoothies – are compliant and complete.

The 5 coolest
SECRET BARS

---

186 COYO TACO
2300 NW 2nd Avenue
Wynwood ③
+1 305 573 8228
coyo-taco.com

One of the speakeasies that started the trend, the Coyo Taco Wynwood location has a door marked 'Employees Only' in the back. Head through it to find a full bar, usually in full swing with a DJ rocking the deck and customers taking to the floor. Tacos, of course, soak up the mezcal.

187 SALONI BAR BY MERAKI
140 SE 1st Avenue
Downtown ④
+1 786 536 2400
salonibymeraki.com

Next door to Meraki Greek Bistro, this cozy space is the opposite of the Greek cliché of white, white, white. Instead, think modern, moody Athens married to the hippie vibe of Meraki island. Inhale the atmosphere with natural wine, craft beers, and lots of *mezze*. Designed for locals, the happy hour is wallet-friendly.

188 FREDDYS SPEAKEASY
AT: INTERCONTINENTAL
MIAMI
100 Chopin Plaza
Downtown ④
+1 305 577 1000
*icmiamihotel.com/
freddys*

This joint, which holds a max of 12 people, is so hidden you need to make an appointment for it (on Open Table) and can only stay for two hours. You're escorted to it and admitted with a secret knock. Then you'll be given a taste of a specialty cocktail. After that, it's up to you what to order.

189 TEA ROOM
AT: EAST MIAMI
**788 Brickell Plaza
Brickell** ⑤
+1 305 712 7000
*easthotels.com/en/
miami/restaurants-
and-bars/tea-room*

Also located in a hotel and speaking to the hotel's roots, this Asian speakeasy is hidden behind a black door. Open it to find a stunning Hong Kong-inspired lounge that showcases the views of downtown, pours craft cocktails infused with Eastern and tropical ingredients, and offers one of the city's only night brunches. Reservations highly suggested.

190 KAONA ROOM
THE HIDDEN TIKI ROOM
**1600 NE 1st Avenue
Downtown** ④
+1 305 800 8454
kaonaroom.com

This side-street speakeasy – or *speaky-tiki* as the owners call it – is a Polynesian throwback. It only allows 45 guests inside at a time. That's probably because it's so stuffed with tiki memorabilia that more can't fit. Be warned if you're not accustomed to tiki culture: These folks pour with a heavy hand.

188 FREDDYS SPEAKEASY

KREL TROPICAL KNITWEAR

70 PLACES TO SHOP

The 5 best
MALLS and
SHOPPING DISTRICTS

---

191 **COCOWALK**

3015 Grand Avenue
Coconut Grove ⑧
+1 786 367 7726
cocowalk.com

This formerly down-and-out multi-story mall is now a refurbished, 150.000-square-foot, indoor-outdoor retail and lifestyle center. This truly is a place 'Where the Grove Comes Together,' offering entities like a French jeweler, free outdoor yoga sponsored by activewear shop FP Movement, and plenty of dining options.

191 COCOWALK

192 ANTIQUES & DESIGN MIAMI

8650 Biscayne Blvd
MiMo District/
Upper East Side ②
+1 305 458 7134
antiquesand
designmiami.com

Not all of the tenants in this 30-plus showroom mural-painted facility are antiques dealers. Some are designers; others sell fine art. But many of these dealers, from all over the world, do specialize in art deco, mid-century and other 20th century collectibles, including Nihil Novi, Worth Galleries, Deco Dreams, and Michel Contessa Antiques.

193 WYNWOOD JUNGLE

50 NW 24th St
Wynwood ③
+1 917 281 0330

With retail and dining that ranges from homegrown Miami clothing boutiques to food halls and rooftop bars to art galleries and design stores, the Jungle is easily recognized by its brightly colored, tropical murals that detail the outside of the building.

194 CAULEY SQUARE HISTORIC VILLAGE

22400 Old Dixie Hwy
Redland ⑭
+1 305 258 3543
cauleysquare.com

Originally built in 1903, these restored cottages were once home to men who worked in a railroad shipping yard. Now they're a charming piece of old Florida, with each tiny home an individual boutique, antique store, wellness center, art gallery, tea room, or restaurant.

195 UPPER BUENA VISTA

184 NE 50th Terrace
Little Haiti ②
+1 305 539 9555
upperbuenavista.com

This charming shopping-and-dining oasis was constructed around the 120-year-old *bodhi* wish tree, fluttering with ribbons upon which guests have written their hopes and dreams. Before or after stopping into any of the micro-boutiques or eateries, stop at The House of Findings for a ribbon of your own.

5 of the best shops for
TRENDY MIAMI
clothing

---

196 U-ROCK COUTURE

928 Ocean Drive
South Beach ⑫
+1 305 538 7625
urockcouture.com

Open since the mid-1990s on Ocean Drive, this rock culture-inspired clothing store – as implied by the double entendre name – offers stud-worthy duds and accessories. In many cases, those are literal studs or other embellishments. Get-you-noticed labels here for men and women include BB Simon, King Baby and Robin. A second location is on Collins Avenue.

197 THE WEBSTER

1220 Collins Avenue
South Beach ⑫
+1 305 674 7899
thewebster.us

Named for the 1935 art deco building in which the flagship store is housed, The Webster is an assemblage of unique designer fashion items for both men and women. Owner Laure Heriard Dubreuil debuted a second Webster in Bal Harbour in 2013.

198 TUPELO HONEY

7250 SW 57th Avenue
South Miami ⑭
+1 305 667 2400

It happens – you look around Miami and realize you're wearing the wrong style of jeans. Style moves fast around here and you gotta keep up, so head to Tupelo Honey to replace your denims. Both men's and women's styles here have kept up with the times since the 1970s. A second location is in Aventura.

199 WYNWOOD TRIBE

2200 NW 2nd Avenue,
Suite #107
Wynwood ③
+1 786 867 7342
wynwoodtribe.com

Funky graphic tees, hoodies and sweaters, jeans and shorts, dresses and shoes, outerwear and swimwear, accessories ranging from wallets to caps… this place truly has it covered for both women and men. As a bonus, it carries all sustainable, fair trade, and up-cycled brands. Another perk: Shop online, pick up curbside.

200 ANATOMIE

6701 NE 4th Avenue
Little River ②
+1 833 576 1900
anatomie.com

If there's two things that people like to do in Miami, it's travel and work out. This is why it makes sense that Anatomie, founded by athleisure vets Kate and Shawn Boyer, would have its headquarters/concept showroom in Miami. Their men's and women's lines are chic enough to don for dinner but casual enough to relax in during the day. Find their clothes at the Miami Beach Carillon pop-up store and in the Mandarin Oriental, Miami.

5 renowned
MIAMI-BASED
FASHION DESIGNERS

---

201 JULIAN CHANG

6733 NE 3rd Avenue
MiMo District/
Little River ②
+1 786 857 6934
julianchang.com

Known for his beautiful tailoring and structured, contemporary, playful looks, Peruvian native Chang has been a longtime favorite for locals. Buy his off-the-rack outfits online or in 600 boutiques around the country. Or make an appointment and head in for a custom-designed cocktail or bridal piece.

202 KREL TROPICAL KNITWEAR

AT: MIAMI IRONSIDE
7580 NE 4th Court,
#111
Little River ②
krelwear.com

Knits look good on everybody, even in the subtropics. Nobody knows that better than designer and textile artist Karelle Levy, who operates 'Maggie,' her industrial knitting machine, making all sorts of lightweight, fashion-forward styles in solids, ombre, and even glitter.

203 NILÜFER BRACCO

niluferbracco.com
niluu.com

Nilüfer Bracco didn't always call Miami home. Nor was she always a designer. But now both are true. And her highly desirable vegan silkwear brand, niLuu, is a responsible choice for those who also love to feel the cooling luxury of beautiful fabrics on their sun-heated skin. Carrried in Neiman Marcus and elsewhere.

204 RAMONA LARUE BY ARIANNE

3400 N Miami Avenue
Midtown ③
+1 305 456 8191
ramonalarue.com

These highly original separates and dresses are a fashionable tribute to designer Arianne Brown's mother, Mona, who taught the Coconut Grove native how to hand-paint silk. Every item begins life as actual art. Then the designs are transferred to flowing clothing, all manufactured in Miami, that sway to the tune of the body.

205 JUST BEE QUEEN

+1 305 517 1265
ext. 101
justbeequeen.com

Actually, it should be Just Bee Queens, plural. That's because this resort wear brand comes to us courtesy of mother-daughter team Maria and Sydney Strauss. Order online or find their flirty separates and sexy silhouettes, inspired by their Cuban heritage, at stockists including Neiman Marcus, Revolve, and Bloomingdale's.

202 KREL TROPICAL KNITWEAR

SHOPS FOR WOMEN

―――――――――

206 VICKY VICTORIA

2401 Biscayne Blvd
Edgewater ③
+1 786 558 4910
vicky-victoria.com

Edgy, spot-on fashion – if you don't have it before you come to Miami, this is where you go to get it. You can outfit yourself from leopard print headband to pastel pink sock boots, or whatever's in style at the time. In Miami, urban glam's the game. Thanks to sisters Victoria and Isabel, we've been able to have it since 2015.

207 MIRO'S BOUTIQUE

7216 SW 57th Avenue
South Miami ⑭
+1 305 667 0084

Elegance awaits at this quality, chic boutique. Whether you're looking for something formal, resort wear, or a piece more appropriate for work-to-date night, you'll find it here. In addition, Miro's carries accessories and hosts trunk shows. Seasonal sales also help you stock up on that perfect outfit. Personalized service is another plus.

208 FRANKIE.

1891 Purdy Avenue
Miami Beach ⑬
+1 786 479 4898
frankiemiami.com

When two BFFs combine their curatorial style instincts, you get this Sunset Harbour shop where locals beeline every season, counting on the fashion savvy of owners Anna and Cheryl. And the ladies never disappoint, stocking frankie. with pieces that range from daytime frilly to downright sultry. Don't forget to check out the jewelry and accessories as well, ranging from shoes to hats to scents.

209 EARTHY CHIC BOUTIQUE

9705 NE 2nd Ave
Miami Shores ①
+1 305 364 5989
earthychic.com

Though Miami might seem all glitz and glamour, it has its boho-chic, resort, and even yoga mom sides, too. Earthy Chic accommodates all of Miami's moods, and yours, too, with a large collection of silhouettes and styles. A great collection of jewelry, handbags, and more help you complete your look-of-the-moment.

210 CATTIVA BOUTIQUE

3205 NE 1st Avenue
Midtown ③
+1 786 309 0068
cattivaboutique.com

From jeans to jackets and swim suits to sweaters, this customer-oriented shop has it all. Unique but on-trend pieces display quality, and the shop is craftily designed, with lovely displays of accessories and sitting areas for guests who are there for approval purposes only.

5 singular
SHOPS FOR MEN

---

211 OFY
171 NW 25 St
Wynwood ③
+1 786 360 6063
ofyshop.com

Founded by third-gen luxe retailer Ofir Farahan when he was 23, Ofy is both a brand and a brick-and-mortar store in Wynwood. Dedicated since 2013 to sustainable practices as much as it is to urban fashion, Ofy offers Miamians no choice between looking good and acting responsibly. When you're a consumer of the cool fashion choices and accessories from footwear to fragrances here, you do both.

212 BASICO WYNWOOD
189 NW 25th St
Wynwood ③
+1 786 360 3688
shopbasico.com

Originally located on South Beach, this store has moved around Miami wherever the scene has become fashionable. You can count on its contents keeping up with the times equally as well. Outfit yourself here from underwear to outerwear and top to bottom from sunglasses to shoes.

213 BASE

2215 NW 2nd Avenue
Wynwood ③
+1 305 531 4982
baseworld.com

For many years a staple on Lincoln Road when South Beach was renovating, BASE moved its flagship store to Wynwood when that region showed regeneration. This should tell you one thing: BASE knows hip in clothing, books, gift items, cologne and other one-of-a-kind items.

214 LOWER EAST COAST

7219 NW 2nd Avenue
Little River ②
lowereastcoast.com

Part cool zine and book store, part indie clothing brand boutique, Lower East Coast reps lines with Miami street cred. In addition to their own brand, find Carhartt W.I.P., Delicate Porcelain, Stray Rats, The Good Company, and more pushing sweats, tees, snapbacks, hoodies, keychains, and even the occasional skate deck.

215 SUPPLY & ADVISE

223 SE 1st St
Downtown ④
+1 305 960 2043
supplyandadvise.com

For the well-groomed guy whose office air-conditioning is set to 60 degrees, or who's visiting from colder climes. Clothing ranges from wool suits to an unusually large sock selection. In fact, you can get everything from pocket squares to gift cards to office goods. This is also one of the few men's stores where you can find items to keep your shoes neat, polished, brushed and clean.

5 awesome
ANTIQUE STORES

---

216 STONEAGE ANTIQUES

3236 NW S River Dr
West Little Havana ⑦
+1 305 633 5114
stoneage-antiques.com

Collecting and selling for more than half a century, this huge, riverside store-front specializes in nautical antiques, and often supplies props for TV and film sets. The inventory is vast, so try taking a virtual tour and then calling in your order. The business might be Stoneage but it's 21st-century tech savvy.

217 ANTIQUE MALL Y'ALL

9845 E Fern St
Palmetto Bay ⑭
+1 305 969 0696
antiquemallyall.co

Why settle for one store when you can shop at more than 100? The dealers here range from specializing in estate sales to consignments to plain old sales of vintage and antique items. Open since 1998 and seven days a week, the mall's agents have goods arriving every day, so you can always discover new-to-you pieces.

218 GALLERIA D'EPOCA

800 NE 125th St
North of Miami ⓵
+1 786 399 4222
galleriadepoca.com

Many antique stores are a hodgepodge collection, but this one has a theme. Born in Parma, Italy, Maria Rosa Bradley has been specializing in luxury Italian collectibles, lighting, furniture, mirrors, jewelry, and handbags since 1999. She favors mid-century designers such as Piero Fornasetti, Fontana Arte, and Gio Ponti, and has new articles arriving daily.

219 WALDANS ANTIQUES & VINTAGE FURNITURE

4209 SW 75th Avenue
Glenvar Heights ⑮
+1 786 399 4446
waldans.com

With items sourced from estate sales and consignors, this showroom is stuffed with elegant couches, china sets, silver, lamps, sconces, chandeliers, vases, glassware, art, and collectibles of every conceivable kind. You wouldn't know it from the bars on the windows and the garish temporary signs, but the items in here are generally clean, high-quality, and organized. They range in age from retro to truly antique, and come from every school and style of decorative arts.

220 TURN BACK THE CLOCK SHOP

6354 Bird Road
South Miami ⑭
+1 305 666 2064

Age-wise, the items in this adorable boutique straddle the line between vintage and antique. But why split hairs when you can have this much fun looking through items that remind you of the Golden Girls? Clothing, jewelry, cameras, cassette tapes, vinyl records, toys, phones, typewriters… you'll feel like you've walked back in time just by walking in.

The 5 most excellent
V I N T A G E *and*
T H R I F T *shops*

---

221 FLY BOUTIQUE

7235 Biscayne Blvd
MiMo District/
Upper East Side ②
+1 786 332 4156

Not just fly but super fly, especially when it comes to vintage designer finds. Every available inch of this spot is hung, stacked, or modeled on a mannequin with some kind of yesteryear YSL, Prada, Chanel, or Gucci treasure. New pieces come in every day and nothing lasts long, so if you see a piece of signed furniture or pair of shoes that you love, BIN. Like they say, nothing lasts forever.

222 MIAMI TWICE

6562 SW 40th St
West Miami ⑮
+1 305 666 0127
miamitwice.com

Opened in the 1980s, this store is an icon in the vintage fashion world. Visit for well-kept pieces from the past whose time has returned, or for that perfect Halloween costume. Owners Mary Kyle Holle and Diane Kyle also know quality, so if collecting luxury labels from bygone eras is your gig, this is your place.

223 THE FASHIONISTA CONSIGNMENT BOUTIQUE

3135 Commodore Plaza
Coconut Grove ⑧
+1 305 443 4331
shopthefashionista.com/#hero

For all your top designer needs, frequent this mother-and-daughter store, in business for more than two decades. Vintage and lovingly used current stock from the world's most fashionable brands, from Balenciaga and Blumarine to Bottega Veneta and 7 For All Mankind, offer a palette for the stylish woman to paint a picture-perfect wardrobe.

224 LOTUS HOUSE THRIFT CHIC BOUTIQUE

2040 NW 7th Avenue
Wynwood ③
+1 305 576 4112
lotushousethrift.org

The mission here is admirable: The thrift shop outfits the homeless women and children who live at the Lotus House shelter; sells the overflowing surplus; and employs the women, allowing them to save money and learn skills for the real world. But come here also because the clothes, coming from wealthy, seasonal closet cleaners, rock.

225 DRAGONFLY THRIFT BOUTIQUE

3141 SW 8th St, Suite A
West Flagler ⑦
+1 833 757 5327
dragonflythrift.org

Run by the Ladies Empowerment and Action Program (LEAP), this thrift store has a purpose: It provides education, mentorship, training, and post-release jobs to incarcerated women. Oh, and it also supplies some pretty cool vintage textiles, kitchenware, furniture, clothes, jewelry, books, and more, donated by affluent members of Miami society.

5 happening
HOME DESIGN *stores*

226 **STRIPE VINTAGE MODERN**

799 NE 125th St
North Miami ①
+1 305 893 8085
*stripevintage
modern.com*

If you want to design a home to look like Miami, then 'vintage modern' are your key words. Which should lead you directly to Stripe's doors, where mid-century modern furnishings and accessories are the mission statement. Sourced from all over the world by owners Eric Cody and Arel Ramos, the furniture and objets d'art are textbook chic.

227 **VISIONNAIRE MIAMI**

2063 Biscayne Blvd
Edgewater ③
+1 786 577 4370
visionnaire-home.com

Visionnaire was founded in Bologna, Italy in 1959 with an emphasis on craftsmanship. Now in Miami, one of only two showrooms in the U.S., the brand features furnishings that would make any home appear palatial. It also includes exclusive couture design installations such as the one from Gustavo Cadile Couture. Even if you live in a tiny home, go in and browse the sumptuous collections for the experience.

228 HOME DESIGN STORE

3750 NW 46th St
Hialeah ⑯
+1 305 633 1355
homedesignstore
florida.com

Can you say Buddhas? These folks can. In fact, they get regular shipment of decorative Buddhas – along with fountains, frogs doing yoga, coyote bar stools, and Indonesian teak benches formed by following the natural shape of the wood. This place also prides itself on finding unusual pieces of furniture and decorative arts from all over the world. You never know what might be in stock – or, on the flip side, gone.

229 THE SHOWROOM

3133 Commodore
Plaza
Coconut Grove ⑧
+1 305 418 0749
theshowroom-
miami.com

Proprietor Marilyn Sanchez, who brings an extensive background in fashion design to the home decor business, treats this store like it was her own house. That means that every single item in here is not just something that she can live with, but loves. From art to bedding to rugs, you'll be sure to love it, too.

230 GLOTTMAN

2213 NW 2nd Avenue
Wynwood ③
+1 305 438 3711
glottman.com

Whether you're looking for big installations (furniture, lighting systems, storage, flooring) or little *objets d'art* and home items, you're going to find a modern, eclectic assortment at architect Oscar Glottman's place. Many will prove irresistible, but there are always new gadgets each time you come back. And if you can't decide how or what fits into your space, ask for help from the designer himself.

The 5 nicest boutiques for
UNUSUAL GIFTS

---

231 KICKED UP MIAMI

1787 SW 67th Avenue
West Miami ⑬
+1 786 212 9973

Shop for the kicks collector in your life! Because it's a sell/buy/consign/trade model, you never know what rare, unusual, or interesting sneakers you're going to find. Brands include Jordan's, Yeezy's, dunks, and more. There's also sports apparel and, for the hungry who have been shopping too long, made-to-order cookies.

232 SWEAT RECORDS

5505 NE 2nd Avenue
Little Haiti ②
+1 786 693 9309
sweatrecordsmiami.com

The first independent vinyl record shop to make its appearance in Miami, Sweat is iconic both for its history and its selection, which runs the gamut. Whether you're looking for a gift for a fan of the fifties or a dedicated millennial stuck in Y2K, you'll find just what you need. Or buy a friend a ticket for the occasional workshop on concert photography or dance party event.

233 GOLDENBAR

3162 Commodore
Plaza
Coconut Grove ⑧
golden.bar

This apparel-meets-accessories-meets-home design store has an offbeat but stylish model that allows you to discover the perfect gift for someone who is always on the leading edge of fashion. The clothing is tony. The accessories range from darling to irreverent. And the home goods are exactly what you weren't looking for but always knew you needed.

234 WALT GRACE VINTAGE

300 NW 26th St
Wynwood ③
+1 786 483 8180
waltgracevintage.com

Check out this odd pairing of cars and guitars for the enthusiast in your life. This gallery of vintage electric guitars and Porsches was named after a John Mayer song, according to owner Bill Goldstein. Buy, sell or trade a guitar here, or if you're super generous, drive away in a dream for the one you love. There is also current and new musical gear.

235 URBEN GIFTS & GADGETS

5802 Sunset Drive
South Miami ⑭
+1 786 577 0151
shopurben.com

Whether you're looking for a fire extinguisher emblazoned with the logo of a designer race car or a toiletries bag featuring the image of a vintage basketball, you'll find it here. This is the store to shop for the person who has everything, unless they already possess both a Golden Girls puzzle and a set of bulldogs doing yoga poses.

5 awesome stores for
SPORTS

236 SOCCER LOCKER

9601 S Dixie Hwy
Pinecrest ⑭
+1 305 670 9100
soccerlocker.com

The international popularity of futbol is reflected in Miami's diverse population. Soccer Locker caters to that obsession with a significant selection of footwear, apparel and equipment. The employees are also happy to share which bars are soccer friendly, where to play a pick-up match, and how to find a club or camp.

237 MIAMI NAUTIQUE

237 MIAMI NAUTIQUE

3828 NW 2nd Avenue
Wynwood ③
+1 305 438 9464
miamiskinautiques.com

For boats, wakeboards and water skis, look no further. This long-running business supplies the equipment you need, plus the wetsuits and life vests so that you can not only slalom the waves, but survive them, too. Yep, even in freestyling Miami, precautions are important, so allow Nautique to kit you out.

238 HIGH FIVE SKATE SHOP

315 Lincoln Road
South Beach ⑫
+1 305 531 6112

Need a deck? Looking for wheels? Have a hankering for helmets and pads? High Five is ready to lend a hand. The store stocks dozens of brands, along with a fashionable selection of skate apparel and videos of professionals showing off their tricks.

239 ROLLER SKATE USA

7340 SW 48 St, #104
Glenvar Heights ⑮
+1 305 668 6001
rollerskateusa.com

Freestyle urban skate. Inline speed skates. Roller derby skates. Ice hockey or artistic figure skates. Even multi-terrain skates. Whatever your need is, you'll find it here. One of the oldest skate companies in Miami, Roller Skate USA started on South Beach in 1998 when the inline skating craze was at its height.

240 PELÉ SOCCER

532 Lincoln Road
South Beach ⑫
+1 786 238 7448
pelesoccer.com

Literally fun and games, this Brazilian soccer player's superstore is covered with turf so that players can test their cleats and balls before buying. It also plans to hold watch parties on custom-built bleachers in the 7000-square-foot store, which stocks jerseys from more than 150 national and international teams.

The 5 best
FLEA MARKETS

241 OPA LOCKA INDOOR FLEA MARKET

13499 NW 42nd Ave
Opa-Locka ⑦
+1 305 688 0500
opalockamarket.com

A tradition in the community for more than four decades, this indoor market offers goods and services from more than 200 vendors. Find electronics, shop for shoes, clothing, and jewelry, buy locally grown plants and produce, or get your hair cut. You can even eat your fill of prepared foods at the food trucks. Open daily from 9 am to 6 pm.

242 REDLAND MARKET VILLAGE

24420 S Dixie Hwy
Redland ⑬ ⑭
+1 305 257 4335
redlandmarket
village.com

Since 1987, this sprawling market – which includes a generous farmers' market – has been enticing visitors to the Redland and Homestead farming regions. In fact, it started with vegetables, and has since expanded over 27 acres to include all sorts of goods, including antiques, leather (especially cowboy boots), tools, toys, and jewelry. Thursday-Sunday.

243 TROPICANA FLEA MARKET

2951 NW 36th St
Allapattah ③
+1 305 316 7594
tropicana
fleamarket.com

Tropicana is one of Miami's longest-running fleas. It's also one of the largest, with 200 vendors selling everything from pet products to auto materials, A food court, farmers' market, and plenty of shoes, clothing and jewelry merchants are enough to keep you occupied for hours – if not all day. Friday-Sunday.

244 LINCOLN ROAD ANTIQUE & COLLECTIBLE MARKET

800-1120 Lincoln Rd
Miami Beach ⑫
antiquecollectible
market.com

For 30 years and counting, various eclectic vendors set up two or three times per month – always on a Sunday – on this well-trod walking mall. If you're a fan of digging through tables of old silver, costume jewelry, vintage games and toys, and retro outfits, then this recurring outdoor market is for you. See the website for specific dates.

245 THE VILLAGE FLEA MARKET & MALL

AT: NORTHSIDE
SHOPPING CENTER
7900 NW 27th Ave
West Little River ①
northsideshopping
centre.com

Just east of Hialeah, this flea market-meets-mall has a lot going for it. To begin with: Air conditioning. Next: More than 100 vendors. And third: Like most flea markets, there's a variety of goods to source, ranging from clothing to jewelry to cosmetics. But you can also get your hair cut at a barbershop or your nails done at a number of salons. Get your shopping done and get a makeover at the same time.

5 bodegas and markets to buy
INTERNATIONAL
NECESSITIES

---

246 MARKY'S GOURMET

687 NE 79th St
MiMo District/
Upper East Side ②
+1 305 758 9288
markys.com

Go ahead – covet the caviar. And the foie gras. And the truffles. The imported goods beckon. But the reality is, you don't have to just browse. For the most part, prices are no higher than at gourmet grocery chains, and there are delicacies that you can't find anywhere else including Marky's own beluga caviar, farmed in northwest Florida.

247 SENTIR CUBANO

3100 SW 8th St
Little Havana ⑧
+1 305 644 8870
sentircubanoshop.com

For all your Cuban needs, from *guayaberas* (shirts) to dominos, trust this long-running store, in business since 1999. What began mostly as a grocery is now a full-service supplier of all Cuban necessities, including décor, souvenirs, musical instruments, essential kitchen tools like a mortar and pestle, and plenty of accessories for cigar aficionados.

248 PUBLIX SABOR

Miami and
Hialeah ⑯
*www.publix.com/
pages/publix-sabor*

Just about every Miamian shops at
a Publix for groceries. But Publix Sabor
is pretty special. Only a few of these pan-
Latin versions exist for the sole purpose
of providing goods to the Hispanic community. They're a great way to familiarize
yourself with the real flavor of the city.

249 BRAZIL MART

18090 Collins Avenue
Sunny Isles Beach ①
+1 786 816 2265

With additional locations in Aventura,
Coral Gables and Doral, Brazil Mart is
a mini-supermarket chain catering to
the large extant Brazilian population in
Miami. That means you can get all the
Brazilian and Portuguese favorites that
you're craving, from *coxinhas* (fried dough
with shredded meat inside) and *pamonhas*
(like Mexican *tamales)* to Brazilian beers
and fresh sugarcane juice to music and
even clothing.

250 LA BODEGA – PERUVIAN RESTAURANT & STORE

13774 SW 88th St
Kendall ⑭
+1 305 386 8836
*labodegarestaurant.
business.site*

You might want to first dine on octopus
in olive sauce, spoonfuls of ceviche or
any of the numerous fish and seafood
dishes first. Then visit the shelves at the
back of the establishment, where you
can purchase sauces, packaged mixes
and Peruvian products to continue the
experience at home.

The 5 best
MIAMI SOUVENIRS

251 MIAMI HEAT JERSEY
AT: KASEYA CENTER
601 Biscayne Blvd
Downtown ④
+1 786 777 3008
themiamiheatstore.com

Like any professional team, the Miami Heat has its ups and downs. But the last decade has seen more of those ups, and even its downs don't seem so low. Celebrate the heart this team displays, no matter who gets traded, by purchasing a jersey at a game. It'll make you feel warm all over.

252 BOTTLE OF MIAMI'S FIRST CITY-DISTILLED RUM
AT: MIAMI CLUB RUM
7401 NW Miami Place
Little River ②
+1 844 642 2582
miamiclubrum.com

The city's first distillery offers hourly tours of its facility; these include tastings of the rum, made with local Florida ingredients. Buy a bottle to bring home (but only if you're checking your bags). The next time you make a mojito, you'll practically hear the rumba in your glass.

253 FEDORAS
AT: HATS & HATS
BY PUERTO FINO HATS
1836 NE 163rd St
North Miami Beach ①
+1 305 944 8202
hatsandhats.net

You can never go wrong in Miami wearing a fedora. Timeless and trendless, it's ideal for anybody, regardless of age or gender. Find the perfect one to take home – material, color, shape of crown and brim – at this establishment, which has 2000-square-feet of headgear available.

254 UNIVERSITY OF MIAMI HURRICANES GEAR

AT: UNIVERSITY OF MIAMI
1306 Stanford Drive
Coral Gables ⑨
+1 305 284 4101
bkstr.com/miamistore/home/en

College sports fans know how mighty the Division I Hurricanes can be. Stop into the bookstore for a commemorative hoodie before watching a home baseball game at 'The U's' Alex Rodriguez Park at Mark Light Field or a basketball game at the Watsco Center. (Note: Football games are played off campus at Hard Rock Stadium.)

255 CIGARS

AT: CUBA TOBACCOO CIGAR CO.
1528 SW 8th St
Little Havana ⑦
+1 305 649 2717
cubatobacco cigarco.com

You have plenty of options when it comes to good Cuban cigars in Miami, especially on Calle Ocho. In fact, it can get confusing. So don't fool around. Head to this family business, operating for more than a century. Whether you're buying for yourself or for someone else, they'll guide you into making the soundest decisions.

253 FEDORAS

5
UNEXPECTED OUTLETS

256 DOLPHIN MALL

11401 NW 12th St
Sweetwater ⑮
+1 305 365 7446
shopdolphinmall.com

It's hard not to feel your heart racing. With more than 240 retailers in one huge setting – many value-oriented – you almost don't know where to go first. Here are some favorites: Banana Republic Factory Store. Bloomingdales's – The Outlet Store. Vans Outlet. Saks OFF 5TH. Swarovski. Try to stay calm.

257 GUESS FACTORY

AT: THE SHOPS
AT MIDTOWN MIAMI
3252 NE 1st Avenue,
#100
Midtown ③
+1 786 453 0336
stores.guess.com

In between Wynwood and Miami Design District, both of which house fairly pricey boutiques, there's Midtown. And in Midtown, there's the outlet for Guess, where you can get a terrific selection of men's and women's clothing and accessories – including sunglasses, shoes, jewelry, watches, wallets and handbags – at great prices. Check online for additional locations.

258 SKECHERS WAREHOUSE OUTLET

AT: MIAMI GATEWAY
805 NW 167th St
North Miami Beach ①
+1 305 627 0535
local.skechers.com

Cute, comfortable, colorful – you can find lots of ways to describe these casual, athletic shoes. But at this factory outlet store, where they stock a healthy selection of both adult and kid sizes, the best one is affordable. Check the online site for electronic coupons and nearby locations, too.

259 PREMIER TABLE LINENS

7321 NW 35th St
Doral ⑯
+1 800 937 1159
premiertablelinens.com

You probably won't be surprised to hear that this is the only table linen factory outlet in the entire country. But given the amount of events that both locals and visitors alike hold in Miami, it makes sense. Go here for everything from tablecloths, napkins and runners to trash can covers, chair sashes, and Christmas tree skirts in a veritable artist's palette of colors.

260 LINEN FACTORY OUTLET

1783 NW 20th St
Allapattah ③
+1 305 325 1905
linen-factory-outlet.
business.site

This outlet sounds like it might offer bed sheets or bath towels. But Linen Factory Outlet refers to the fabric, not the product. Located near Wynwood, it actually features bright, comfortable and fashionable women's wear at reasonable prices.

THE VAGABOND HOTEL

20 BUILDINGS
TO ADMIRE

The 5 most amazing
ART DECO
renovations

---

261 THE COLONY THEATRE

1040 Lincoln Road
South Beach ⑫
+1 305 674 1040
miaminewdrama.org

With its unmistakable movie marquee and streamlined, geometric architecture rising behind it, The Colony is one of the last original buildings on Lincoln Road. It debuted as Paramount Pictures in 1938 and underwent a 6,5-million-dollar restoration 80 years later. Since 2016, it has been the home of nonprofit professional theater group Miami New Drama.

262 HOTEL BREAKWATER SOUTH BEACH

940 Ocean Drive
South Beach ⑫
+1 305 532 2362
breakwater southbeach.com

Architect Anton Skislewicz designed this emblematic structure in 1936. Formerly pastel, it is now a magnificent blue-and-orange façade, with the enormous neon sign that spells out the name of the hotel fronting the parapet, and vertical lines shooting out from the sides of the frieze.

263 MIAMI CITY HALL

3500 Pan American Drive
Coconut Grove ⑧
+1 305 250 5400
miamigov.com

This was Pan American Airlines' airport for the famous flying seaplanes. The 1934 building featured interior murals and a stunning, curved canopy. Many of the art deco elements were hidden with a bland redo in 1954 when it became City Hall, but it was restored to its former self in 2003.

INTERNATIONAL PIANO
FESTIVAL DISCOVER SERIES 2017

261 **THE COLONY THEATRE**

264 MIAMI BEACH POST OFFICE

1300 Washington Ave
South Beach ⑫
+1 305 672 2447
tools.usps.com/
find-location.htm?
location=1372882

With a large circular rotunda serving as the lobby and wings extending to either side, this is unmistakably art deco. It was designed by Miami local Howard Lovewell Cheney and built in 1937, with a three-panel mural added above the gold post office boxes in 1940. Overhead, a light fixture painted like the sun shines down on a fountain.

265 COLONY HOTEL

736 Ocean Drive
South Beach ⑫
+1 305 673 0088
colonymiami.com

This art deco restoration has dominated every skyline since South Beach reinvented itself. The bright blue neon signage, the flat roof with more neon enlivening it, the tri-level division. It's earned its place in the postcards.

5 *stunning*
MEDITERRANEAN
REVIVAL *buildings*

266 **CORAL GABLES CITY HALL**

405 Biltmore Way
Coral Gables ⑨
+1 305 446 6800
coralgables-fl.gov

Given that this planned community site was finished in 1928, at the height of the architectural trend, it makes sense to visit it for those notable features: stuccoed walls, roof tiles, clock tower and, most strikingly, its frontal Corinthian colonnade. Designed by Phineas Paist and Harold Steward, it was created from limestone quarried nearby.

267 **HOTEL ST. MICHEL**

162 Alcazar Avenue
Coral Gables ⑨
+1 305 444 1666
hotelstmichel.com

Part of George Merrick's Spanish-Mediterranean 'City Beautiful', this lodging was built in 1926 and originally called the Sevilla Hotel. Today the boutique property, with its stucco, carved stonework, wrought iron detailing and balconies, is still a lovely place to stay. Already have a place? Dine at the elegant Zucca Ristorante and explore the property.

268 VIZCAYA VILLAGE

ACROSS: VIZCAYA
MUSEUM & GARDENS
3251 S Miami Avenue
Coconut Grove ⑧
+1 305 250 9133
vizcaya.org/collections/
vizcaya-village/about-
vizcaya-village

Vizcaya, James Deering's bayfront mansion, is a Mediterranean Revival masterpiece of its own. The Vizcaya Village, where his staff lived and worked, is a continuously restored and improved part of the estate. These 11 buildings, from 1916, are now used for cultural/arts programming, horticulture and native conservation, and urban farming.

269 OLYMPIA THEATER

174 E Flagler St
Downtown ④
+1 305 575 5057

A stunning piece of architecture in downtown Miami, the Olympia began life as a silent movie theater in 1926, and later became respected for both Vaudeville and air-conditioning. It's also been known, at various points of restoration, for its interior turrets and towers, a ceiling painted like a night sky, balconies and a courtyard.

270 THE VILLA CASA CASUARINA

1116 Ocean Drive
South Beach ⑫
+1 786 485 2200
vmmiamibeach.com

This over-the-top boutique hotel and restaurant was constructed in 1930 by adventurous architect Alden Freeman, who modeled the home after the Alcazar de Colon, even using a brick from it that he brought back. It was purchased by Gianni Versace in 1992, who renovated and added more gilded features; Casa Casuarina was also where he was tragically killed.

5 Miami modern
MOTELS

---

271 SINBAD MOTEL MIAMI

6150 Biscayne Blvd
MiMo District/
Upper East Side ②
+1 305 751 3110

Designed by Tony Sherman to resemble a ship – because the bay was visible then from the property – this blocky 1953 motel, complete with brise-soleils and winged overhangs, was named after Sinbad the Sailor. Its instantly recognizable neon signs, which remain today, are featured in the 1995 movie *Miami Rhapsody*.

272 NEW YORKER BOUTIQUE HOTEL

6500 Biscayne Blvd
MiMo District/
Upper East Side ②
+1 786 913 0680
*thenewyorker
miami.com*

Showcasing the neon signs and angular façade, this hotel is in the hands of the family who have owned it since the 1980s. Renovated (with lots of flamingo decor) in 2009 to keep up with the changing MiMo District landscape, they solicit a clientele interested in quiet quality and offer a funky, outdoor happy hour in the courtyard.

273 SHALIMAR MOTEL

6200 Biscayne Blvd
MiMo District/
Upper East Side ②
+1 305 751 0345
*shalimarmotel
miami.com*

Architect Edwin Reeder designed this motel in 1951, and it stood apiece with the ramshackle others until a complete redo was accomplished in 2013. Streamlined with community balconies and MiMo accents – including the signature neon sign – it offers clean, reasonably priced lodging.

274 THE VAGABOND HOTEL

7301 Biscayne Blvd
MiMo District/
Upper East Side ②
+1 305 400 8420
*thevagabond
hotelmiami.com*

With its futuristic asymmetry and angularity, The Vagabond was a vision of Miami Modern. Designed in 1953 by Robert Swartburg, it was a magnet motel/lounge for the Rat Pack. Today it has been thoroughly reinvented and modernized, with a chic pool scene, casual Mediterranean eatery and more.

275 THE BISCAYNE HOTEL

6730 Biscayne Blvd
MiMo District/
Upper East Side ②
+1 305 456 0432
thebiscaynehotel.com

Renovated and very mid-century modern, this boutique hotel has come back from a derelict past. You can stay for a night or two or a more extended amount of time. Enjoy the clean lines, rooms that are surprisingly generous in size, and a lobby that is neat and chic. Within walking distance to many services and restaurants.

274 THE VAGABOND HOTEL

5 of the most
ICONIC MIAMI MASTERPIECES

—————

276 FREEDOM TOWER
AT: MIAMI DADE COLLEGE
600 Biscayne Blvd
Downtown ④
+1 305 237 7700
mdcmoad.org/
freedom-tower

One of the most culturally meaningful landmarks in the city, this model of Seville's Giralda Cathedral Bell Tower was built in 1925. Its history includes being used to process Cuban exiles from 1962 to 1974 – thus its nickname. It originally housed The Miami News, and now hosts the MDC Museum of Art + Design.

277 FONTAINEBLEAU MIAMI BEACH
4441 Collins Avenue
Miami Beach ⑪
+1 800 548 8886
fontainebleau.com

Perhaps the most compelling example of futuristic MiMo architecture, the 'curvilinear' Fontainebleau was designed by legendary architect Morris Lapidus in 1954. As glamorous now as it was then, the 22-acre beachfront property is an attraction for global celebrities, professional athletes and cognoscenti.

278 THE BASS
2100 Collins Avenue
South Beach ⑫
+1 305 673 7530
thebass.org

Designed by Russell Pancoast in the 1930s, this unique art deco contemporary art museum was first a public library. In 2017, it reopened with a 12 million-dollar expansion of its exhibition and program spaces, cafe and a museum store, while still making use of its historic galleries.

279 HIALEAH PARK RACING & CASINO

100 E 32nd St
Hialeah ⑯
+1 305 885 8000
hialeahparkcasino.com

Glitzy and lavish with balustrades and curving staircases, this 1920s Mediterranean Revival structure, set on 200 acres, is as captivating as it is entertaining. It's the only race course listed on the National Register of Historic Places and, because of its flock of resident flamingos, originally brought over from Cuba, as an Audubon Bird Sanctuary.

280 MIAMI TOWER

100 SE 2nd St
Downtown ④
miamitower.net

This signature 47-story skyscraper lights up in different colors or patterns to suit the occasion, be it a holiday, a season or even a Dolphins game. A graduating, three-tiered glass spire that rises above a 10-story parking garage, this office building was originally built for CenTrust Bank.

276 FREEDOM TOWER

BRICKELL AVENUE

40 PLACES
TO DISCOVER
MIAMI

———

5 awesome
VIEWS OF DOWNTOWN

---

281 RUSTY PELICAN

3201 Rickenbacker
Causeway
Key Biscayne ⑥
+1 305 361 3818
therustypelican.com

Soaring sea birds. Boats whose sails fly just as high. And an encapsulated view of downtown Miami. That's what you see when you perch at the Rusty Pelican, which underwent a 7 million-dollar renovation in 2011 and later unveiled a wine menu featuring more than 300 bottles. Sip, stare and sink into bliss.

282 SUGAR

AT: EAST MIAMI
788 Brickell Plaza
Brickell ⑤
+1 786 805 4655
east-miami.com

This rooftop lounge and garden puts the 'scene' in scenic. Crowning the 40th floor, it features 360-degree views of the downtown region and the water – although you'll have to tear yourself away from the lush landscaping and Asian tapas in order to take it all in.

283 VELA SKY

AT: YOTEL MIAMI
227 NE 2nd St
Downtown ④
+1 786 785 5700
vela-miami.com

When the sun is high in the sky, so should you be, swimming in the rooftop pool and gazing over the skyscrapers toward Biscayne Bay. And when it starts to set, sip on a cocktail, snack on some light bites, and channel the neon rays while vibing to some beats. There's no better way to experience Miami.

284 MATHESON HAMMOCK PARK

9610 Old Cutler Road
Coral Gables ⑨
+1 305 665 5475
*www.miamidade.gov/
parks/matheson-
hammock.asp*

Sit on the family-friendly beach and watch your little ones wade in the atoll pool. Behind them, kite boarders soar against the pinks and golds of late-afternoon sun, striking off the skyscrapers of distant downtown Miami. You couldn't ask for better Instagram snaps.

285 VENETIAN CAUSEWAY

A series of 12 bridges (10 fixed, 2 bascule) connecting 11 islands from Downtown to South Beach ③⑫
*www.miamidade.gov/
parks/venetian.asp*

The sights from these low-rising bridges, located northeast of downtown, are outstanding during the day. But thanks to the architects who built Miami and their penchant for adding neon hues to various skyscrapers, some of the coolest illuminations of the scene are at night.

285 VENETIAN CAUSEWAY

The 5 nicest
WATER VIEWS

---

286 WATR AT THE 1 ROOFTOP

AT: 1 HOTEL SOUTH BEACH
2341 Collins Avenue
Miami Beach ⑪
+1 305 604 6580
1hotels.com/south-beach

Wearing core coastal grandmother, this Japanese-inspired venue certainly takes advantage of its view. And what a view it has of the Atlantic and its beaches in all their stunning glory. Sunset drinks here are a social media feed must. But don't worry if the day turns gray. Watr has a retractable roof to keep you dry.

288 PIER 5

287 KLAW MIAMI

1737 N Bayshore Dr
Edgewater ③
+1 305 239 2523
klawrestaurant.com

Located in the historic Miami Women's
Club, Klaw offers the finest in Norway's
king crab claws. Relish them and the
fabulous view of Biscayne Bay, seen
through floor-to-ceiling windows, at the
same time. Then head up to the only
rooftop in Edgewater for some more
saltwater breeze and a nightcap.

288 PIER 5

AT: BAYSIDE MARKETPLACE
401 Biscayne Blvd
Downtown ④
+1 305 209 0090
pier5.com

Located within Bayside Marketplace, Pier
5 is a whirlwind of activations, food and
drink options, DJ sets, and live music –
all happening on the lip of Biscayne Bay.
This place opens up just as the sun sets,
offering you a chance to dance to the
rhythm of both the Miami night and the
ocean waves.

289 THE KAMPONG

4013 S Douglas Road
Coconut Grove ⑧
+1 305 442 7169
*ntbg.org/gardens/
kampong*

Listed on the National Register of Historic
Places, The Kampong is an incredible
collection of historic fruit cultivars and
flowering trees, many of them from
Southeast Asia. The tropical oasis leads
down to sparkling panoramas of Biscayne
Bay. Book a tour or reservation in advance.

290 JULIA TUTTLE CAUSEWAY/ INTERSTATE 195

4,4 miles
connecting I-95
to Miami Beach,
Edgewater to
Miami Beach ③⑪

Miami is famous for being flat as paper,
but the Julia Tuttle rises above – literally.
As one of the causeways connecting the
mainland to the beaches, it can almost
be called a hill. At the crest, drivers can
see the Atlantic, dotted with mangrove
islands and water craft, extending on
both sides.

5 great
NEIGHBORHOODS

---

291 **ESPAÑOLA WAY**
HISTORIC DISTRICT
South Beach ⑫
visitespanolaway.com

This historic, pedestrian-only boulevard was originally designed as an artists' colony in the 1920s and frequented by notables in the field such as Kenny Scharf, Desi Arnaz, Miralda and Craig Coleman. It was redeveloped and relaunched in 2017 by Craig Robins, who modeled the design after Barcelona's Las Ramblas.

292 **BRICKELL**
Brickell Avenue and associated streets, Downtown Miami
Brickell ⑤

The bustling, beating heart of the downtown business district, Brickell Avenue and its connecting side streets – commonly shortened to simply 'Brickell' – is a cosmopolitan collection of condominiums, luxury hotels, restaurants, bars and assorted retail establishments.

293 **BIRD ROAD**
ART DISTRICT
7259 SW 48th St
Olympia Heights ⑮
+1 305 467 6819
thebirdroad
artwalk.com

Previously, this industrial tract, located by railroad tracks, was filled with warehouses. Artists began converting those buildings into studios in the 1980s. The District now includes galleries, art schools, and stages for live theater, music, and spoken word performances.

294 LITTLE HAITI

The southern border North (NW/NE) 54th St, west to Interstate 95 and north along the Miami city boundary on North (NW/NE) 80th St; East (NE) 2nd and 4th Ave ②

Home to the many immigrants from Haiti and other Caribbean islands, Little Haiti (and its neighbor, Little River) is also an up-and-coming arts-and-entertainment district. Galleries, boutiques and restaurants are moving in next door to traditional Caribbean eateries and shops. It's a colorful and evocative blend that locals hope will keep its character as it develops.

295 MIMO BISCAYNE BLVD
HISTORIC DISTRICT
MIMO BISCAYNE ASSOCIATION
8101 Biscayne Blvd, #309-310
MiMo District/ Upper East Side ②
+1 786 391 3993
mimoboulevard.org

Short for Miami Modern, the MiMo District is also known as the Upper East Side. It encompasses a swath of Biscayne Boulevard and the neighborhoods of Morningside and Shorecrest, which contain wonderful examples of mid-century modern architecture. Once a desolate strip, today the MiMo District is a thriving, resurgent community.

291 ESPAÑOLA WAY

The 5 most beautiful
BOTANIC GARDENS

296 THE JOHN C. GIFFORD ARBORETUM

UNIVERSITY OF MIAMI
AT: 231 COX
SCIENCE CENTER
1301 Memorial Drive
Coral Gables ⑨
+1 305 284 1302
arboretum.as.
miami.edu

Take your time strolling through and relaxing in this teaching and research facility. These 500 or so species of tropical plants and trees, originally collected and nurtured in 1947, have survived multiple hurricanes and other catastrophes. Its University of Miami campus scientist caretakers, who use it for educational purposes, welcome visitors for self-guided tours.

297 PINECREST GARDENS

11000 Red Road
Pinecrest ⑭
+1 305 669 6990
pinecrestgardens.org/
botanical

Pinecrest Gardens takes its plants pretty seriously, offering horticulture workshops for those who not only admire the collections here but also want to work with them elsewhere. Still, this 'cultural arts park' also features tons of entertainment: concerts, theater and dance performances, holiday-themed festivals such as 'Howl-O-Ween', family movie nights and Sunday farmers' markets.

297 PINECREST GARDENS

298 CASTELLOW HAMMOCK PRESERVE & NATURE CENTER

22301 SW 162nd Ave
Redland ⑬⑭
+1 305 242 7688
www.miamidade.gov/
parks/castello-
hammock.asp

If you've always wanted the chance to scout for owls at night, you've got one. This is just one of the activities you can sign up for at this 112-acre preserve, which contains a mature tropical hardwood forest that is very popular for birds and butterflies, and those human beings who like to watch them.

299 CERVECERÍA LA TROPICAL

42 NE 25th St
Wynwood ③
+1 305 741 6991
cerveceria
latropical.com

Long story short: Established 1888 in Cuba, this brewery was the oldest on the island, and included famous tropical gardens. Fast-forward to Miami where a fifth-generation family member persuaded Heineken to open this joint venture in 2020. Take a seat in history, drink some refreshing ale, eat some fabulous fare and tour the gardens, planted in partnership with Fairchild Tropical Botanic Garden.

300 MIAMI BEACH BOTANICAL GARDEN

2000 Convention
Center Drive
South Beach ⑫
+1 305 673 7256
mbgarden.org

This historic site was originally created as the 'Garden Center' in 1962. After suffering from Hurricane Andrew, it was revitalized in 1996 by the Miami Beach Garden Conservancy. Free and open to the public, it now offers everything from orchids to koi ponds, and sponsors arts and cultural programming such as the Japanese Spring Festival.

5

HISTORIC BEACHES

301 HISTORIC VIRGINIA KEY BEACH PARK

4020 Virginia
Beach Drive
Virginia Key ⑥
+1 305 960 4600
*virginiakey
beachpark.net*

Established as the 'Colored Only' beach in 1945, this mile-long shoreline contains an antique carousel as well as the oldest plant and animal varieties – many endangered – in the region. View them on the restored hammock trails and wooden boardwalk. Virginia Key also offers a mini train, a modern playground and a Tiki Village for amenities.

302 BILL BAGGS CAPE FLORIDA STATE PARK

1200 S Crandon Blvd
Key Biscayne ⑥
+1 305 361 5811
*floridastateparks.org/
parks-and-trails/bill-
baggs-cape-florida-
state-park*

The oldest building in Miami-Dade County – a lighthouse constructed in 1825 – stands on these sands, which were also a stop on the Underground Railroad. A regularly recognized 'top ten' beach in the nation, BBCFSP is a rest-and-eat stop for the neotropical birds that migrate through; birders as well as sunbathers and fishermen find this paradise.

303 HAULOVER PARK

10800 Collins Avenue
Bal Harbour ⑩
+1 305 947 3525
*www.miamidade.gov/
parks/haulover.asp*

Although it was purchased in 1935, Haulover wouldn't be developed completely until 1947 because of WWII. Many myths account for the name, ranging from Prohibition bootleggers to a barefoot mail carrier, all who 'hauled over' items to the mainland before roads were built. Today the beach is famous for flying kites and its nude bathing section.

304 SOUTH BEACH

Ocean Drive,
betw 5th and 15th St
South Beach ⑫
miamiandbeaches.com

South Beach began as a coconut farm in 1870, and was developed for residences starting in 1910. A decade later, the wealthy poured in for sunshine, bringing with them the art deco architects who left their lasting marks on Ocean Drive, where restoration of these landmark hotels began in the late 1980s and continues today.

305 SURFSIDE

Collins Avenue,
betw 87th and 96th St
Town of Surfside ⑩
townofsurfsidefl.gov

One mile long, this classic beach town, a loggerhead turtle sanctuary, was frequented by celebrities like Frank Sinatra, Elizabeth Taylor and Winston Churchill. They stayed at the Surf Club, opened in 1930 by tire tycoon Harvey Firestone; today it's a revitalized Four Seasons property where Thomas Keller debuted his first Miami establishment in 2018.

5 *terrific*
GUIDED TOURS

---

306 MIAMI BREW BUS
2003 N Miami Avenue
Wynwood ③
+1 786 558 3860
miamibrewbus.com

Want to tour local breweries? Every Saturday, Miami Brew Bus offers three options, each of which include lots of samples (starting at pick up!), a souvenir glass and more. Tour times vary in the afternoon and evening and cost 97 dollar per person plus taxes and fees (prices liable to change). Note: Closed-top shoes required; must be 21+.

307 MIAMI SEAPLANE TOURS
555 NE 15th St, #17
Downtown ③
+1 305 361 3909
miamiseaplane.com

It's not every day that you take in Miami via both water and sky. But Miami Seaplanes allows you to do just that. Book half-day or full-day tours or charters for guided sightseeing, in conjunction with curated activities, or for quality aerial chauffeuring to nearby destinations such as Key West.

308 LITTLE HAVANA FOOD & CULTURAL TOUR

WITH: MIAMI CULINARY TOURS

MEETING POINT: TOWER THEATER

1508 SW 8th St
East Little Havana ⑦
+1 303 578 6877
*miamiculinary
tours.com/tour/little-
havana-food-tour*

The best way to get acclimated to a new city is through your stomach. Since Miami is largely Cuban, you should start by taking a tour of Miami's Cuban eateries. But no matter what tour you choose to take, you'll always find yourself in Robyn Webb and her operators enthusiastic, hospitable hands.

309 SEGWAY AND BIKE TOURS

WITH: BIKE & ROLL

210 10th St
South Beach ⑫
+1 305 604 0001
bikeandroll.com

This company has a lock on the wheels. If you crave some exercise, sign on for a guided bicycle tour of, say, Wynwood or South Beach. Feeling lazy but want the cooling breezes? Size up a Segway and join a group for an informative ride.

310 KAYAK FISHING TOURS

WITH: IPADDLE MIAMI

AT: PELICAN HARBOR

1275 NE 79th St
North Bay Village ⑩
+1 305 472 3353
*ipaddlemiami.com/
kayak-fishing-tours*

It's one thing to paddle around Miami in a kayak, getting some exercise and taking in the view. It's another thing entirely to do it while fishing. iPaddle offers both freshwater and saltwater fishing, supplying both guides and gear. They specialize in snook and peacock bass, but will schedule any freshwater and inshore saltwater trip to catch what you want to catch.

5 *top*
TATTOO PARLORS

---

311 OCHO PLACAS TATTOO COMPANY

4703 SW 8th St
Flagami/
Little Gables ⑨
+1 305 264 0888
ochoplacastattoo.com

Founded in 2001 by Jose Carreras, who passed away in 2009, this Calle Ocho shop has been carried on by his former employees, John Vale and Javier Betancourt. Now sought after by celebrities, the skilled inksters at Ocho Placas are in high demand, but the artists themselves remain a humble, hometown crew.

312 FAME TATTOOS

1409 W 49th St,
Suite 1
Hialeah ⑯
+1 305 303 2025
*fametattoos.com/
realistic-color-tattoos*

These are some wild, realistic and incredibly detailed tattoos, inscribed by fervid artistes. The shop and staff reflect an aesthetic of Prohibition chic – slightly naughty but always modish with more than a dash of panache. If you want a tattoo along with a real Magic City experience, Fame is the place to get it.

313 IRIS

2700 N Miami Ave,
#508
Wynwood ③
+1 786 615 9186
iris.tattoo/miami

Stunning 3D designs, pastel inks and delicate lines define some of the styles at Iris Tattoo. But that's not all that differentiates this place, which feels more like a friend's stylish, comfy apartment than a typical tattoo parlor. Clean, minimalist, striking, and modern, this studio promises – and delivers – a holistic experience.

314 ALEX CHIONG TATTOO STUDIO

12949 Biscayne Blvd
North Miami ①
+1 786 613 0486
alexchiong
tattoostudio.com

This clean and stylish shop looks like a well-proportioned hair salon, reflecting owner and artist Alex Chiong's years of experience in the field. Here, he and his team of artists do a large variety of styles, including color realism, black and gray realism, watercolor, tribal, new school, and Japanese, as well as piercings.

315 TATTOO & CO.

AT: MIDTOWN MIAMI
TOWER 2
3449 NE 1st Ave, #110
Midtown ③
+1 305 485 0770
tattooandco.com

In business since 2003 – which in Miami years is like the lifetime of 10 dogs – this shop is certified, sterilized, and clean, clean, clean. And they want to make sure you get what you want. So call them to consult, customize a drawing, and arrange for anything from a celebrity likeness to scalp micropigmentation. Body piercing is also available.

5 of the best places to
SPOT CELEBRITIES

---

316 PAPI STEAK

736 1st St
South Beach ⑫
+1 305 800 7274
papisteak.com

Because of its everyday opulence –
which includes the option of ordering
a $1000 steak that's served in a beefcase
(a play on the word briefcase) with literal
bells, whistles, and even a branding
iron – David Grutman and David 'Papi'
Einhorn's 90-seat steakhouse hosts its
share of celebrities. These include Venus
and Serena Williams, Bad Bunny, and
Eva Longoria.

317 SEXY FISH MIAMI

1001 S Miami Avenue
Brickell ⑤
+1 305 889 7888
sexyfishmiami.com

This over-the-top, ocean-motif restaurant,
which celebs already loved in London,
was a shoo-in for sightings in Miami.
So far, Lady Gaga, Drake, Margot Robbie,
Rafael Nadal, Jimmy Butler, Jamie Foxx,
and others have been spotted among
the mermaid dancers, international
DJs, popping Champagne corks, and
popular signature dishes like duck salad,
vegetarian sushi, smoked tuna belly,
and black cod.

318 FORMULA 1 CRYPTO.COM MIAMI GRAND PRIX

AT: HARD ROCK STADIUM

347 Don Shula Drive
Miami Gardens ①
+1 305 943 7223
f1miamigp.com

This three-day racing event, which is supported by parties all over the city, is a huge draw for A-listers. Scout all the famous participants and onlookers, from performers like Shakira and the Jonas Brothers to actors including Tom Cruise, James Marsden, and Vin Diesel to athletes like Shaq and Patrick Mahomes.

319 ART BASEL MIAMI BEACH

AT: MIAMI BEACH CONVENTION CENTER

1901 Convention
Center Drive
South Beach ⑫
+1 786 276 2600
artbasel.com/miami-beach

This international visual arts festival transforms the South Beach and the main corridor of Miami into a progressive party (and traffic) jam. Luminaries from every medium – art, film, music, sports and literature – show up to perform, host, curate or simply appear at charity events, gallery walks, product releases and museum showcases. While many of the events are private or require a ticket, others are open to the public.

320 FOOD NETWORK SOUTH BEACH WINE & FOOD FESTIVAL

VARIOUS LOCATIONS

South Beach ⑫
sobewff.org

This delicious festival, held over the last weekend of February, has something for everybody: bring your kids (to family events) or club kids (21+). Celebrities hosting events range from actors, musicians, and athletes hawking their wares (Dwyane Wade, Adam Levine, Eva Longoria, Kate Hudson) to Food Network stars (Guy Fieri, Snoop Dogg, Martha Stewart) to TikTok, YouTube and Instagram influencers.

TOWER THEATRE

80 PLACES TO ENJOY CULTURE

The 5 most important
SMALL GALLERIES

---

321 MARKOWICZ FINE ART

**110 NE 40th St
Miami Design
District ②
+1 786 615 8158**
markowiczfineart.com

Never boring and always diverse, this gallery has exhibited a range of art from pop to street by well-known, international artists such as Andy Warhol and Jean Cocteau. Represented artists include American Carole A. Feuerman, Dutchman Johannes Boekhoudt, Canadian Jonah Waterous and South African Neill Wright.

322 DINA MITRANI GALLERY

**2620 NW 2nd Avenue
Wynwood ③
+1 786 486 7248**
dinamitranigallery.com

This eponymous gallery features a global roster of renowned photographers, including Peggy Levison Nolan, Rafael Diaz, Roberto Huarcaya, Kanako Sasaki and Tatiana Parcero. Mitrani is also a force in the local community, creating opportunities out of her father's former clothing factory.

323 MINDY SOLOMON GALLERY

**848 NW 22nd St
Allapattah ③
+1 786 953 6917**
mindysolomon.com

Specializing in emerging and mid-career artists, this lovely space is run by a practising artist, dealer, collector, educator and advocate. As a result, the paintings, photography, sculptures and videos are exhibited in meaningful relationships to each other.

324 VALLI ART GALLERY

1924 N Miami Avenue
Wynwood ③
+1 305 747 5287
valliartgallery.com

Founder Franco Valli's mission is to promote Italian-American art. To that end, he curates pieces by Italian artists, and works closely with them so that he is able to comprehensively communicate with the viewer the meaning of their pieces.

325 LOCUST PROJECTS

3852 N Miami Avenue
Miami Design
District ②
+1 305 576 8570
locustprojects.org

This not-for-profit space encourages wide-ranging, site-specific installations from artists anywhere – regional, national and international – and presents them as free, educational opportunities to the public. The organization was founded by Miami artists Elizabeth Withstandley, Westen Charles and COOPER, and was one of the first to spot potential in the neighboring Wynwood area.

321 MARKOWICZ FINE ART

The 5 coolest places for
PUBLIC ART

---

326 **MIAMI-DADE COUNTY CHILDREN'S COURTHOUSE**
155 NW 3rd St
Downtown ④
+1 305 679 1600
jud11.flcourts.org/
About-the-Court/
Miami-Dade-Childrens-Courthouse

Find the 186-foot-long *Urban Quilt* by ceramicists Carlos Alves and JC Carroll in the courtyard. Inside, Tom Otterness' *Familia de Osos,* an installation of bears and humans, acts out a court session. Murals by Roberto Juarez are scattered throughout the lower floors. And Jackie Chang's glass panel triptych deconstructs the word 'just.'

327 **ARTS AVENTURA MALL**
AT: AVENTURA MALL
19501 Biscayne Blvd
Aventura ①
+1 305 935 1110
aventuramall.com/arts

Cartsen Höller's twisty *Aventura Slide Tower* is both fun and functional art. Another popular spot for public art is in the midst of the *Gorillas in the Mist,* sculpted by twin brothers Nikolai and Simon Haas. These are just two examples of the two dozen pieces of public art at this popular luxury mall.

328 THE UNDERLINE

**The Underline
Brickell Backyard
Brickell ⑤**
theunderline.org/art

A 10-mile linear trail that follows underneath Miami's Metrorail, The Underline will feature public art the whole way. In the River Room and Promenade sections, you can find permanent sculptures *Bronze* by Hank Willis Thomas and *Water/Tables* by Cara Despain. Other sections, such as the Fern Room, Oolite Room, Promenade, and Metromover/Metrorail stations, feature rotating temporary public sculptures.

329 MIAMI-DADE PUBLIC LIBRARY SYSTEM

VARIOUS LOCATIONS
*mdpls.org/art/
permanent-collection*

Miami-Dade Library's permanent public art collection began in the 1970s. It contains about 3000 pieces from 900 or so artists, mostly representing Latin America and the Caribbean. Their pieces are installed throughout the entire system, with individual artist's collections occasionally brought out for exhibits. Each branch also displays temporary exhibits as well as special sessions with musicians, poets, and other local creatives.

330 HARD ROCK STADIUM

**347 Don Shula Drive
Miami Gardens ①
+1 305 943 8000**
*media.hardrock
stadium.com/art*

In 2016, when the Hard Rock Stadium renovation was revealed, the public was surprised to see that Dolphins owner Stephen Ross was committed to adding artistic value to the venue. After partnering with Goldman Global Arts (GGA), the stadium has 19 murals by 18 artists from 10 different countries. Check the website for the location of the pieces so that you know before you go.

5 *of the best places for*
PERFORMING ARTS

---

331 SANDRELL RIVERS THEATER
6103 NW 7th Avenue
Little Haiti ②
+1 305 284 8800
sandrellrivers
theater.com

Named for artist and arts advocate Chief Sandrell Rivers, the theater is devoted to dance and other events that have struggled to find their place in Miami. It's managed by Fantasy Theatre Factory, a company devoted to youth audiences, and The M Ensemble Company, Florida's longest-running African American theater organization, is the resident company.

332 WESTCHESTER CULTURAL ARTS CENTER
AT: TROPICAL PARK
7930 SW 40th St
Westchester ⑫
+1 305 226 0030
wcacenter.org

A 200-seat black-box theater, this flexible space with a lobby art gallery opened in 2022. Its focus is Hispanic arts and culture in Southwest Dade. The resident theater group, The Roxy Theatre Group, is aimed at kids ages 3-17, offering classes in dance, drama and voice as well as the opportunity to perform in stage productions.

333 DENNIS C. MOSS CULTURAL ARTS CENTER

10950 SW 211 St
Cutler Bay ⑭
+1 786 573 5316
smdcac.org

From ballets by local dance companies to concerts by long-running Latinx acts, this official venue, known colloquially as The Moss Center, is a great place to catch events that reflect the city's diversity. The South Dade facility, built to fine arts specifics in 2011, also offers education and outreach programs.

334 ACTORS' PLAYHOUSE AT THE MIRACLE THEATRE

280 Miracle Mile
Coral Gables ⑨
+1 305 444 9293
actorsplayhouse.org

Founded in 1988, this professional theater company performs a full season tailored for the community in a renovated historic venue. It offers live productions for both its 600-seat Mainstage and Children's matinee programs, and each is typically critically acclaimed and award winning. There's also a 300-seat Balcony and a 100-seat Black Box theater.

335 MIAMI THEATER CENTER

9806 NE 2nd Avenue
Miami Shores ①
+1 305 751 9550
mtcmiami.org

Here, resident company Mad Cat Theatre Company and others invited by MTCproductions/MTCpresents entertain the region with a range of performances, from originals to adaptations and poetry to puppetry on the MainStage. Next door, new work is hashed out at the black-box theater in the SandBox Series. Films screened in partnership with O Cinema.

5 exciting

INDEPENDENT CINEMAS

---

336 O CINEMA
1130 Washington Ave
South Beach ⑫
+1 786 471 3269
o-cinema.org

If you're craving an independent film, art flick, international film, documentary on a musician, or black-and-white classic, then O is it. If you're in town for a while, check out the membership; if you can't make it out to the theater, look into the virtual option that you can use to stream.

337 SILVERSPOT CINEMA
300 SE 3rd St, #100
Downtown ④
+1 305 536 5000
downtownmiami.
silverspot.net

See an independent or foreign film, an opera or ballet – or yes, a typical Hollywood blockbuster – while you recline with a glass of wine, some miso-glazed salmon and a piece of five-layer chocolate cake for dessert. Want to host a private screening or plan a meeting, party or event? You can arrange to do that here as well.

338 CORAL GABLES ART CINEMA
260 Aragon Avenue
Coral Gables ⑨
+1 786 385 9689
gablescinema.com

This large, modern theater is a collaboration between the City of Coral Gables and the nonprofit Coral Gables Cinematique. One of the more comfy spots to see first-run, independent features and documentaries, international films and classics. It also shows the Annual Miami International Children's Film Festival.

339 TOWER THEATER

1508 SW 8th St
Little Havana ⑦
+1 305 237 2463
towertheater
culturalcenter.com

The Tower debuted as an English-language cinema in 1926, but switched to Spanish when Cuban *exilios* arrived. It got a new lease on cultural life in 2002. Now an independent cultural center, it screens Spanish- and English-language films and sponsors exhibits, lectures, performances, poetry readings and more.

340 THE BILL COSFORD CINEMA

AT: UNIVERSITY OF MIAMI
SCHOOL OF COMMUNICATION
5030 Brunson Drive
Memorial Building 227
Coral Gables ⑨
+1 305 284 9838
cosfordcinema.com

Serving both the university and the greater population for more than 60 years, this cinema shows a variety of formats, from 35 mm to high-definition digital. Both an educational experience and an art facility, it brings in international film festivals and engagements with renowned filmmakers Chantal Akerman, John Landis and Andy García.

339 TOWER THEATER

The 5 best public places to
BRING YOUR PUP

---

341 PÉREZ ART MUSEUM MIAMI (PAMM)
1103 Biscayne Blvd
Downtown ④
+1 305 375 3000
pamm.org

While dogs aren't allowed inside where the Latin American and Caribbean artwork is, they are allowed anywhere outside. That includes the Brazilian green heartwood deck where the 67 sustainable hanging gardens, created by Patrick Blanc, are made up of 54.700 plants comprising 77 different species. What a *sniffari!* They can also have lunch with you at Verde, the museum's waterside restaurant.

342 BRICKELL CITY CENTRE
701 S Miami Avenue
Brickell ⑤
+1 786 465 6533
brickellcitycentre.com

When you want to dine and/or shop and it's too hot out for the pooch, head into the shade offered by the different sections of this open-air, four-level plaza. You can take well-behaved dogs in and out of the high-end, air-conditioned boutiques and cafes, which also have plenty of outdoor seating for pups and their humans. It also offers *pawsome* coverage when it rains.

343 BARNACLE HISTORIC STATE PARK

3485 Main Highway Coconut Grove ⑧
+1 305 442 6866
floridastateparks.org/
parks-and-trails/
barnacle-historic-
state-park

This was the home of Ralph Middleton Munroe, a sea captain who built his estate in 1891 facing Biscayne Bay. One of Miami's oldest preserved properties, it offers tours of the building and replicas of his boats as well as concerts, walking paths, picnic spots and more. The pooches are allowed to *pawtrol* everywhere except inside.

344 HOBIE ISLAND BEACH PARK

South end Key Biscayne (north side of Rickenbacker Causeway) Viriginia Key ⑥
+1 305 361 2833

For the diehard water dogs and their wet-suited pals, Hobie Beach is a natural, dog-friendly strip of sand where the animals are welcome to play in the surf. So are the people. Just be aware that this beach is nicknamed Windsurfer Beach because of the long-running concession that rents out gear as well as its stiff breezes, so the swimming sees a lot of competition with board sports.

345 NIKKI BEACH

1 Ocean Drive South Beach ⑫
+1 305 538 111
miami-beach.
nikkibeach.com

This global brand first opened in Miami in 1998, and we have a soft spot for its blend of hospitality, music, entertainment and, well, beachiness. Why? Because you can enjoy all of it with your furry friend. Whether you want to sit down for brunch, relax on the sand in a cabana or rosé all day in a teepee while vibing to tune, your dogs are welcome to perk up their ears with you.

5 inspiring
SPECIALTY MUSEUMS

---

346 MUSEUM OF ILLUSIONS

536 Lincoln Road
South Beach ⑫
+1 305 604 5000
miaillusions.com

You might as well call this the Instagram Museum. Designed with social media in mind, the 40-plus 3D exhibits encourage you to take wild pictures for your stream. The interactive scenes are inspired by cartoons, current events, famous art, recognizable films and more. It's a lot of fun, if a bit dizzying, both in person and reliving it afterward.

347 BLACK POLICE PRECINCT COURTHOUSE AND MUSEUM

480 NW 11th St
Overtown ⑦
+1 305 329 2513
historicalblack
precinct.org

Too often overlooked, African-American history is preserved here with a special mission in mind: to record the challenges and accomplishments of the Black police officers who were on duty pre-Civil Rights era. Displays feature the bicycles they used, Black Precinct jail cells, original plaques, historic photos and more from the 1940s, 1950s and 1960s.

348 JEWISH MUSEUM OF FLORIDA – FIU

301 Washington Ave
South Beach ⑬
+1 305 672 5044
jmof.fiu.edu

Before any group that currently defines the immigrant experience appeared and settled in Miami, there were the Jews. This museum is dedicated to their culture and history of worldwide discrimination. Exhibits range from amusing (food, fashion) to truly chilling (genocide).

349 WINGS OVER MIAMI AIR MUSEUM

AT: MIAMI EXECUTIVE
AIRPORT
14710 SW 128th St
Kendall ⑭
+1 305 233 5197
wingsovermiami.com

Plane buffs love this place, which is located in a hangar on a runway. An homage to the history of flight, the 'exhibits' include vintage aircraft from the military, civilian and commercial realms, and almost all of them can fly. Most flight activity takes place on weekends.

350 WORLD EROTIC ART MUSEUM

1205 Washington Ave
South Beach ⑫
+1 305 532 9336
weam.com

It makes sense that sexy South Beach would be the home to the only museum in the U.S. dedicated to fine erotic art. It was founded on the personal collection of Naomi Wilzig. Today the museum showcases more than 4000 pieces, dating from 300 BCE to the present.

5 awesome
ARTS FAIRS

---

351 **SOMI ART FEST**
Sunset Drive,
betw U.S. Highway 1
and SW 57th Avenue
South Miami ⑭
+1 305 769 5977
somiartfest.org

This juried show features more than 100 artists from all over the world working in such diverse mediums as ceramics, digital art, textiles, glass, metalwork and photography. If you can conceive it, you can bet it will be there. Free and open to the public, the event includes culinary and musical entertainment.

352 **ART MIAMI**
AT: ONE HERALD PLAZA
At NE 14th St on
Biscayne Bay betw
the Venetian and
McArthur Cwys
Downtown ④
artmiami.com

More than 75.000 lovers of 20th-and 21st-century art visit this fair, which was established in the late 1980s. It showcases galleries and artists and attracts dealers and curators from all over the world during what is now commonly known as Art Week, during Art Basel.

353 CONTEXT ART MIAMI
AT: ONE HERALD PLAZA
At NE 14th St on Biscayne Bay betw the Venetian & McArthur Cwys Downtown ④
+1 305 517 7977
contextartmiami.com

This sibling to Art Miami debuted in 2012 in order to present emerging and mid-career talent, as well as those artists outside the mainstream. It takes place during Art Week, and attracts more than 80.000 people. Park in the garage across the street and hop on shuttles to go between various Art Week fairs.

354 AQUA ART MIAMI
AT: AQUA HOTEL
1530 Collins Avenue South Beach ⑫
+1 305 517 7977
aquaartmiami.com

Scheduled during Art Week, this art fair – related to Art Miami – is set in the boutique Aqua Hotel. The intimate format of rooms-turned-galleries, and crowds spilling into the lush courtyard, makes the contemporary art, brought by more than 45 representatives, even more inviting.

355 RED DOT MIAMI
AT: MANA WYNWOOD
2217 NW 5th Avenue at NW 22nd St Wynwood ③
+1 216 225 0962
redwoodartgroup.com/red-dot-miami

While this fair also takes place during Art Week, it sets itself apart by offering more interactive opportunities for its audience. The art includes all genres and mediums, and features performance pieces, installations, Art Labs, Spotlight Galleries, Directors' Picks, and the Discoveries Collection. Also listen to the Art Fair Confidential podcast, and visit its sister fair, Spectrum Miami.

The 5 most amazing
MUSIC FESTIVALS

---

356 **MIAMI MUSIC WEEK**
VARIOUS LOCATIONS
miamimusicweek.com

Although it's not exactly a secret, the week-long celebration of EDM called Miami Music Week (MMW) is ever-evolving, and you never know what's going to happen. Several years ago, homegrown Ultra Music Festival merged with MMW to become the grand finale, and stayed that way ever since. Overall, it's a highly anticipated week with many satellite events attended by thousands.

357 **III POINTS**
AT: MANA WYNWOOD
**318 NW 23rd St
Wynwood** ③
iiipoints.com

This multi-day, Miami-born festival combines musical performances from eclectic international groups such as Polo & Pan, Kenny Beats, La Femme and Sama' Abdulhadi with new, experiential technology exhibits and grand-scale visual art installations. Being on the showgrounds every October is so multisensory and multidimensional, it's like living in a virtual reality game. Musical acts subject to change.

358 MAKE MUSIC MIAMI
VARIOUS LOCATIONS
makemusicmiami.org

Taking place every solstice, Make Music Miami (MMM) is mmm, good. Called Fête de la Musique in Paris, it began there in 1982; Miami followed suit in 1997 in partnership with the French Embassy. Now also in collaboration with Olympia Arts MIAMI, Buskerfest Miami and The Rhythm Foundation, more than 50 MMM events take place all over the city and are live-streamed if the weather is uncooperative.

359 MIAMIBASH
AT: KASEYA CENTER
601 Biscayne Blvd
Downtown ④
+1 786 777 1000
kaseyacenter.com

Alex Sensation's MiamiBash is a celebration of Latin trap, reggaeton, and Spanish-language R & B. It's billed as Florida's Biggest Urbano festival. The lineup changes every year, but guests could include Ozuna, Manuel Turizo, Kiko El Crazy, Natti Natasha, Ivy Queen, Nio Garcia and Gente de Zona, to name several.

360 MIAMI BEACH CLASSICAL MUSIC FESTIVAL
VARIOUS LOCATIONS
miamimusicfestival.com

With performances all over Miami, the MMF, which launched in 2013, is a summer celebration of young classical musicians. From early June until late July, international applicants from conservatories and universities perform in full operas, symphonic concerts, piano concerts, recitals, chamber orchestra and musical theater performances.

The 5 best
STREET FAIRS

---

361 **CALLE OCHO FESTIVAL**
SW 8th St
(12th to 27th Avenue)
Little Havana ⑦
+1 305 644 8888
carnavalmiami.com

Since 1978, the Kiwanis Club of Little Havana produces this huge March event that celebrates Hispanic culture. Live music, colorful costumes and competitions – who has the best Cuban sandwich or *croqueta?* – attract record-breaking crowds that dance down the street annually. Expect distinctly tropical drinks, too! Carnaval on the Mile, a separate Kiwanis-sponsored fair, takes place a week earlier on Miracle Mile.

362 **MIAMI BOOK FAIR**
AT: MIAMI-DADE COLLEGE, WOLFSON CAMPUS
600 Biscayne Blvd
Downtown ④
+1 305 237 3258
miamibookfair.com

Founded in 1984, this week-long event, one of the most noteworthy in the country, takes place every third weekend of November. Throughout the week, renowned authors read to packed rooms. Over the weekend, the street fair sprawls over several city blocks, with stalls of books and products everywhere and a children's section for the young ones. Subsequent MBF workshops and master classes take place throughout the year.

363 THE KING MANGO STRUT

AT: THE STREETS OF COCONUT GROVE

Coconut Grove ⑧

kingmangostrut.org

Uniquely Miami, this avant-garde parade started in 1981 as a sarcastic response to the Orange Bowl tradition. Now, with its satire well established, the party outdoes itself with self-deprecating, jesting protests. Anything funny goes, and anyone can apply to participate. While alcohol isn't served, the restaurants along the route all participate by selling specialty cocktails.

364 ART DECO WEEKEND

Ocean Drive, betw 5th and 13th St

South Beach ⑬

+1 305 672 2014

artdecoweekend.com

Since 1978, South Beach has been celebrating the art, architecture and era that define its Historic District every mid-January. Activities include tours of Ocean Drive and Collins Avenue, classic car shows, exhibits and lectures, and of course plenty of vendors offering items for sale. There's even an Art Deco Dog Walk!

365 VIERNES CULTURALES

AT: CALLE OCHO

SW 8th St, betw 13th and 17th Avenues

Little Havana ⑦

+1 305 643 5500

viernesculturales.org

This amazing celebration of Cuban arts and culture takes place every third Friday of the month in the fresh air of Little Havana. Enjoy domino games, cigar rolling, live music, dancing, food, arts and crafts, and more. It's a scene that you think can't be repeated – but is, every month.

5 small venues for
LIVE MUSIC

---

366 **MAGIC 13 BREWING CO.**

340 NE 61 St
MiMo District/
Upper East Side ②
magic13brewing.com

The magic here is as much in the details as it is in the events. Grab a house-made Islander lager or MiMo wheat beer. Order tuna *tataki*, grilled octopus, or a *churrasco* sandwich. Then head out into the beer garden to hear whatever band is playing live that night. Follow on social media for advance notice.

367 **MIAMI BEACH BANDSHELL**

7275 Collins Avenue
North Beach ⑩
+1 786 453 2897
miamibeach
bandshell.com

This MiMo jewel of an amphitheater, built in 1961, is part of the North Shore Historic District. Renovated in 2011, it's run by the Rhythm Foundation, which books acts ranging from indie Latin American singer-songwriters to samba. Before a show, have a seat at Bandshell Park's dominoes pavilion or stroll the Beach Walk.

368 THE BACKYARD
AT: THE DORAL YARD
8455 NW 53rd St, #106
Doral ⑯
+1 305 744 5038
thedoralyard.com/live-music

An outdoor extension of The Doral Yard's main dining arena, The Backyard features a live stage and covered turf with plenty of self-serve seating. Live music every weekend ranges from jazz to Latin funk, with plenty of local acts. There's also a large screen for movies and sports events. A bar and Santo Dulce! Churros are also outdoors so that you don't have to go back inside for a snack. And a garden by Little River Cooperative adds vibes.

369 MARTHA / MARY CONCERTS
AT: LA MERCED CHAPEL & CORPUS CHRISTI CHURCH
3220 NW 7 Avenue
Allapattah ③
+1 305 458 0111
marthamaryconcerts.org

For decades, St. Martha's Church has presented reliably awesome global programming in the fields of classical and jazz music at 'movie ticket prices'. Now located in a Spanish baroque chapel and larger adjacent church, it continues outreach to schools and community; no one is turned anyone away for inability to pay. If you can't go in person, tune in live on YouTube.

370 THE GIBSON ROOM
2224 Coral Way
Shenandoah Park ⑦
+1 305 570 4311
thegibsonroommiami.com

This unaffected joint is an ode to chef-owner Michael Beltran's childhood neighborhood. Go here for the vinyl nights and the live music, always a stimulating time. But don't leave without sampling as many of the craft cocktails and as much of the inventive menu from this award-winning chef as you can.

5

NIGHTCLUBS *and* LOUNGES

---

371 MYNT LOUNGE

1921 Collins Avenue
South Beach ⑫
+1 305 532 0727
myntlounge.com

It's no secret that this long-running nightclub, luxe to the max, has one of the strictest door policies in town. If you want to dance to house music under those LED strobes with the other nightlife *hoi polloi*, it's dress – or in the case of South Beach, un-dress – to impress.

372 LA OTRA MIAMI

55 NE 24th St
Wynwood ③
+1 305 908 9368
laotramiami.com

Open Thursday-Saturday from 11 pm-5 am, this Latin nightclub is all about the moves – yours and everyone else's. Ok, and the music. Well, and the outfits, too. Yes, and also the drinks. Put all of those things together to make it a party, Miami-style, which is an experience like none other.

373 MR. JONES

320 Lincoln Road
South Beach ⑫
+1 305 602 3117
mrjonesmiami.com

One of the most decadent nightclubs on South Beach, Mr. Jones has kicked it up so high the partying is stratospheric. For aficionados who know their DJs, Purge Tuesdays and Varsity Fridays are all about hip-hop. But it's the themed, music-driven bottle service parades that grab the attention of drinkers and listeners alike.

374 MAD CLUB WYNWOOD

55 NE 24th St
Wynwood ③
+1 786 843 7021
madclubwynwood.com

If you appreciate a nightclub that greets you with a glass of bubbly instead of a bouncer, then get MAD. Represented by the symbol of a bee, MAD is all about the hive that surrounds it. Become one of its guests and you'll also find an artistically stunning interior as well as DJs such as Alec Monopoly, Marshmello, and Fedde Le Grand. Additional entertainment includes an ever-changing line-up of singers and musicians. Celebs like Anitta, Nicky Jam and Lele Pons party here. But if you missed them, don't get MAD – get a VIP table.

375 BRICK

187 NW 28th St
Wynwood ③
+1 786 467 1205
brickmia.com

Miami's top-rated DJs and standard weekly events, from Uptown Thursdays to Saturday Brunch to Social Sundays, are the big draw here. Graffiti art on the outside of the building; beats and craft beers of all nationalities inside, plus cocktails that change with the seasons – such as they are in the subtropics. A full kitchen open late means you can line your stomach and stay even longer.

The 5 best
LITERARY VENUES

---

376 BOOKS & BOOKS

265 Aragon Avenue
Coral Gables ⑨
+1 305 442 4408
booksandbooks.com

Consistently named one of the best independent bookstores in the country, Mitchell Kaplan's Books & Books sets the stage for every writer in town or who comes through on tour. It hosts more than 60 events per month, from best-selling politicians to YA authors. Additional locations around the city.

377 TEA & POETS

AT: THE SHOPS
AT SUNSET PLACE
5701 Sunset Drive
South Miami ⑭
+1 786 216 7201
teaandpoets.com

Ready to hear some slam beats? How about a sonnet or two? Or a piece of flash fiction followed by a folk song? You never know who might be performing at an open mic here, but the name indicates that it just might be a literary star-in-the-making – or at least one who is practicing diligently.

378 NATIONAL YOUNGARTS FOUNDATION

2100 Biscayne Blvd
Edgewater ③
+1 305 377 1140
youngarts.org

This fantastic organization is all about recognizing and awarding young – as in teenage – talent, and then supporting it thereafter. Hear the literary arts honorees read their work during YoungArts week in Miami, and watch for workshops and performances by these emerging voices at partner organizations in Miami and beyond.

379 BOOKLEGGERS LIBRARY
AT: BAKEHOUSE
ART COMPLEX
561 NW 32nd St
Midtown ③
bookleggerslibrary.com

Non-profit organization Bookleggers is a mobile library that gives you a book every time you see it (and also sells rare books online) as an act of community-building. Feel free to engage it in trades, buy additional books at low cost or make donations. Watch for its multimedia Bookbike, which has speakers and Wi-Fi for performances.

380 THE BETSY – SOUTH BEACH
1440 Ocean Drive
South Beach ⑫
+1 844 862 3157
thebetsyhotel.com

Not only is this historic hotel a luxurious tribute to times gone by, it's a bastion in the literary community. Books are in the rooms, public art is dedicated to poetry, and poets enjoy residencies in the Writer's Room. To that end, there's always a reading, lecture or literary event of some kind going on.

376 BOOKS & BOOKS

The 5 best seasonal
FESTIVALS *and* EVENTS

---

381 SANTA'S ENCHANTED FOREST
7400 NW 87th Avenue
Medley ⑯
+1 305 892 9997
santasenchanted
forest.com

This carnival may be themed around the idea of Christmas, but it's a long holiday. Beginning in November, you can take advantage of more than 100 rides, games and shows. The trees, lights and decorations, which have only been getting more elaborate since the early 1980s, are attractions in themselves.

382 WYNWOOD OCTOBERFEST
AT: WYNWOOD MARKETPLACE
2250 NW 2nd Avenue
Wynwood ③
+1 305 461 2700
wynwood
octoberfest.com

More than a decade old, Wynwood's Octoberfest is celebrated in September. But that's okay – it's also spelled with a 'c.' We don't care as long as there's beer, and there is plenty of that. Presented by Samuel Adams, the three-day festival features seasonal brews, hearty eats, games like *hoist the stein* (part of the Brewlympics), a yodeling contest and plenty of other autumn fun. You won't even notice it's still 90 degrees in Miami.

383 MIAMI SWIM WEEK

AT: VARIOUS LOCATIONS

miamiswimweek.net

Every summer, locals who can stand the heat – and a city stuffed with beautiful people – stick around for Swim Week. That's when dozens of independent designers from Brazil, Italy, Dubai, Toronto, Los Angeles and Miami present their designs to industry titans. In addition to the formal fashion festival, satellite events run the gamut from multi-media runway shows to cocktail parties in chic hotel lobbies and art galleries.

384 HOUSE OF HORROR HAUNTED CARNIVAL

AT: MIAMI INTERNATIONAL MALL

1625 NW 107th Ave Doral ⑯

houseofhorror carnival.com

The largest haunted house experience in South Florida, this annual carnival offers four different scary sections to experience: Mayhem Museum, Haunted HoliDAZE, Theater of Terror and Scare X Studios. Brave it if you must! And definitely applaud the creativity if you're still standing. Rides, food and games are all a thrill. The park opens in late September and runs through Halloween.

385 EASTER DAY EGGSTRAVAGANZA

AT: TRAZ POWELL STADIUM - KIPP MIAMI NORTH CAMPUS

11380 NW 27th Ave Westview ①

It's not an egg hunt unless the eggs are dropped by a helicopter. That's the premise for this community event, hosted by Florida Power & Light and a local radio station. Along with the unusual egg drop, there's a Kid Zone with rides and games, live shows, plenty of vendors for food and treats (and even haircuts!), and lots of colorful candy to go around. Sign up for free every year at EventBrite.

5 places to experience
LATIN CULTURE

---

386 KOUBEK CENTER
AT: MIAMI DADE COLLEGE
2705 SW 3rd St
Little Havana ⑦
+1 305 237 7750
koubekcenter.org

This historic mansion and its gardens were acquired by the city's public college with a specific mission in mind – to promote the Spanish-American diaspora through the arts. The structure was turned into stages, galleries, literary arts opportunities and lecture halls. Now, from films to children's theater classes, there's plenty Spanish-American learning going on.

**387 CUBAOCHO MUSEUM
& PERFORMING
ARTS CENTER**
1465 SW 8th St, #106
Little Havana ⑦
+1 305 285 5880
cubaocho.com

More like a gallery than a museum, as the exhibits continually change, this enterprising business model takes advantage of all its space to also display a large collection of Cuban memorabilia. In addition to live music performances, the venue hosts lectures and book launches, and sells fine art prints in its shop.

388 CISNEROS FONTANALS ART FOUNDATION

1018 N Miami Avenue
Downtown ④
+1 305 415 6343
cifo.org

Called CIFO, this ambitious institution launches for the season every September with a new exhibit under the auspices of its Grants and Commissions Program Collection. The contemporary Latin American artists, either emerging, mid-career, or established, are selected to expose them to curators, collectors and others with influence who visit the Miami art world.

389 AMERICAN MUSEUM OF THE CUBAN DIASPORA

1200 Coral Way
Coral Way ⑥
+1 305 529 5400
thecuban.org

This museum tells the story of the Cuban revolution through art. The exhibits reveal just how heartbreaking it is to leave family, friends and homeland behind forever, and they also show the challenges and the joys of discovering new lives in far-flung places – all through the medium of visual arts. Exile explained; brilliance realized.

390 MÁXIMO GÓMEZ PARK

801 SW 15th Avenue
Little Havana ⑦
+1 305 859 2717
miamigov.com/parks

Casually nicknamed 'Domino Park' because of the number of older Cuban men who play the game there, this neighborhood spot has become quite a colorful attraction. Benches were added a couple of years ago for those who want to watch the action, which can get intense; domino-themed tiles were also installed. There's also a Little Havana Paseo de las Estrellas (Walk of the Stars) which are awarded to Latin celebrities.

5 sites for understanding
HAITIAN HERITAGE

---

391 **HAITIAN HERITAGE MUSEUM**
4141 NE 2nd Avenue, #105-C
Little Haiti ②
+1 305 371 5988
haitianheritage museum.org

This flourishing institution was born in 2004 as an educational platform to connect Haitian Americans with their artistic, historic and cultural roots. The exhibits, films, readings, lectures and musical performances allow every visitor to dig deeply into Haiti's impactful heritage.

392 **LITTLE HAITI CULTURAL COMPLEX**
212-260 NE 59th Terrace
Little Haiti ②
+1 305 960 2969
miamigov.com/ LHCC/home

There are so many wonderful components to this performing arts center, exhibition space, outreach and education space, and community hall. Programming ranges from music and dance concerts to art openings to book festivals, as well as Caribbean Market Days.

393 **LIBRERI MAPOU**
5919 NE 2nd Avenue
Little Haiti ②
+1 305 757 9922
mapoubooks.com

This bookstore stocks work in several languages, including Creole and French, and promotes it by partnering with Miami Dade College to present The Little Haiti Book Festival. It also highlights Haitian arts and crafts.

394 HAITIAN COMPAS FESTIVAL

AT: FPL SOLAR
AMPHITHEATER AT
BAYFRONT PARK
301 Biscayne Blvd
Downtown ④
+1 305 945 8814
haitiancompas
festival.com

Branded just before the turn of the Millennium, this festival – one of the biggest Haitian music events in the nation – gets better every year. Look for top konpa acts like Klass, Nu Look, Ekip, King Street, and more to perform over a several-day period every May. Musical acts and venue subject to change.

395 TOUSSAINT LOUVERTURE MEMORIAL STATUE

6136 N Miami Avenue
Little Haiti ②

Commissioned by the City of Miami, the seven-foot-tall statue of General Toussaint Louverture stands in a small park at the corner of N Miami Avenue and 62nd Street. The Haitian icon, who led the revolution against the French colonists to free the country, is often the site of peaceful demonstrations and vigils.

5 sites for admiring Miami's
NATIVE AMERICAN
background

---

396 **MICCOSUKEE CASINO & RESORT**

500 SW 177th Avenue (Krome Avenue) Everglades ⑬
+1 305 222 4600
miccosukee.com

Sure, you can stack your Bingo cards, try your hand at high-stakes poker, and pull the arm on plenty of gaming machines. But what's really interesting here are all the displays of Miccosukee culture that exist in between the entertainments. The authentic exhibits are just a glimpse of what's been preserved, and what's been lost.

398 MIAMI CIRCLE

397 MICCOSUKEE CULTURAL EXPERIENCES
AT: VARIOUS LOCATIONS
miccosukee.com/resort/experiences

Take an airboat ride to see how the Miccosukee have camped on a hammock in the Everglades for more than 100 years. Discover their respect toward the alligator via various demonstrations. Visit the Village Museum for exhibits that educate about early First Nations and Aboriginal life, then to the Village Gift Shop to take some crafts home with you.

398 MIAMI CIRCLE
AT: BRICKELL POINT SITE
401 Brickell Avenue
Brickell ⑤
trailoffloridas indianheritage.org/miami-circle

This Tequesta archaeological artifact was discovered during preparation for building a skyscraper in downtown Miami in 1998. It dates back to 2000 years before the arrival of the Spanish. No one's entirely sure of the purpose, but it's been preserved so that everybody can take a gander and a guess.

399 HISTORYMIAMI MUSEUM
101 W Flagler St
Downtown ④
+1 305 375 1492
historymiami.org

Find fascinating tribal artifacts in the 37.000-item Object Collection of this reliable museum. In the Seminole Collection in particular, dolls, beads, baskets, patchwork and even wooden dugout canoes are on exhibit. It's a glimpse into the Florida way of life before the Europeans and air-conditioning invaded.

400 PAHAYOKEE OVERLOOK
AT: EVERGLADES NP
Everglades ⑬
nps.gov/ever

The Miccosukee and Seminole tribes called the Everglades home long before they were forced onto government-designated reservations. Visit Pahayokee (Seminole for 'grassy river'), a boardwalk and lookout tower, to gain some perspective and photograph some of the best views.

miami **children's** museum
THE POTAMKIN FAMILY BUILDING

20 THINGS TO DO WITH CHILDREN

The 5 best places with
WILDLIFE

---

401 ZOO MIAMI
THE MIAMI-DADE
ZOOLOGICAL PARK
AND GARDENS
12400 SW 152nd St
Deerwood ⑭
+1 305 251 0400
zoomiami.org

Feed giraffes, parrots or an Indian rhino. Journey down the Asian River Life exhibit. Catch the lion pride at rest; the lowland gorillas in action. Whatever you do, plan your day – this is 750 acres of cage-less space for more than 500 animal species, the fifth largest (but only subtropical) zoo in the country.

402 JUNGLE ISLAND
1111 Parrot Jungle
Trail
Watson Island ④
+1 305 400 7000
jungleisland.com

Jungle Island offers interactive encounters with sloths, kangaroos, flamingos, capybaras, lemurs and giant tortoises. Make the absolute most of it by booking a VIP tour for extra dollars. You can also merely observe if you wish, which is both free (aside from admission fee) and priceless.

403 MONKEY JUNGLE
14805 SW 216th St
Redland ⑭
+1 305 235 1611
monkeyjungle.com

This 30-acre preserve was started in 1935 with just six Java macaques. Now more than 300 primates, many endangered, live expansively in what is essentially a curated rainforest while the humans walk through on protected boardwalks. Watch the Java troupe, now numbering in the 90s, dive for food in their pond.

404 THE ORIGINAL COOPERTOWN AIRBOAT

22700 SW 8th St
Everglades ⑬
+1 305 226 6048
coopertown
airboats.com

Guided airboats, steered by knowledge-able guides, skim over sawgrass in mere inches of water in search of native flora and fauna. You can spot everything from great blue herons to alligators. Afterward, dine on frog legs, alligator and catfish in the on-site restaurant for an additional authentic experience.

405 PELICAN HARBOR SEABIRD STATION

AT: PELICAN HARBOR MARINA
1279 NE 79th St Cwy
North Bay Village ⑩
+1 305 751 9840
pelicanharbor.org/
seabirdcruise

Learn about native and non-native wildlife and the impact of invasive species at this rescue and rehab facility for injured and orphaned wildlife. Founded in 1980, the facility keeps a running tally of the nearly 40.000 treated patients. To help, take a sunset or moonlight seabird cruise or a webinar on conservation with the knowledgeable staff. Funds go to the animals.

404 THE ORIGINAL COOPERTOWN AIRBOAT

The 5 best family
BEACHES, WATER-
PARKS and POOLS

---

406 VENETIAN POOL

2701 De Soto Blvd
Coral Gables ⑨
+1 305 460 5306
coralgables.com/
attractions/
venetian-pool

Chiseled from a limestone quarry pit and complete with grottos and waterfalls this freshwater pool is every child's pirate/princess fantasy playground. There are gorgeous backdrops for sunbathing, selfie-taking teens, and historic architecture highlights for adults. On the National Register of Historic Places. Kids must be 3+. Seasonal attraction.

407 TIDAL COVE

AT: JW MARRIOTT MIAMI
TURNBERRY RESORT
& SPA
19999 W Country
Club Drive
Aventura ①
+1 786 279 6152
tidalcovemiami.com

This water park, which opened at an Aventura resort in 2020, has everything both kids and adults could want. Lazy river? Check. Wave pool? Yes. Slides and fountains and buckets that dump water on your head? Of course. Best of all, there are 25 cabanas and a quick-serve restaurant/market where you can find plenty of option for picky young 'uns who won't get out of the pool anyway. So enjoy your salad and gelato.

408 GRAPELAND WATER PARK

1550 NW 37th Avenue
Flagami ⑦
+1 305 960 2950
miami.gov/Parks-
Public-Places/Parks-
Directory/Grapeland-
Water-Park

Four attractions provide something for everyone. Shipwreck Island is for little ones while Pirate's Plunge is for older kids, but both provide slides, water cannons and splash fountains. Captain's Lagoon is a large, heated pool; the Buccaneer River Ride offers a relaxing float on an inflatable tube. Free life vests available; swim diapers for purchase. Seasonal attraction.

409 MCDONALD WATER PARK

7505 W 12th Avenue
Hialeah ⑯
+1 305 818 9164
www.hialeahfl.gov/731/
McDonald-Water-Park

In addition to the mandatory activity pool, this park features a 305-meter lazy river that takes its riders, ensconced on inner tubes, through a tunnel under a waterfall. A wave pool is also the only of its kind in Miami-Dade County. Catch your breath or consume snacks from the concession at umbrella-shaded tables. Seasonal attraction.

410 MIAMI WATERSPORTS COMPLEX

AT: AMELIA EARHART PARK
401 E 65th St
Hialeah ①
+1 305 476 9253
miamiwatersports
complex.com

This 'Get Up' cable system guarantees that anyone can learn to wakeboard, waterski, wakeskate and kneeboard – even if you don't exactly know what those are. Similar activities are available when being pulled by a boat, along with tubing, and a 10.000-square-foot aquapark with 35 features offers three different skill levels. With lifeguards watching, it's also fun and safe for everyone.

5 fun
PARKS, PLAYGROUNDS
and MUSEUMS

411 MIAMI CHILDREN'S MUSEUM

980 MacArthur Cwy
Watson Island ④
+1 305 373 5437
*miamichildrens
museum.org*

This creatively crafted facility is pure entertainment. Exhibits weave the natural environment, the arts and the multicultural community together. Explore a cruise ship. Bring drawings to life in a virtual aquarium. Shop at a play supermarket or operate a crane at the Port of Miami.

412 LOT 11 SKATEPARK

301-349 NW 2nd St
Downtown ④
+1 754 300 9912
skatefree.org

Sponsored by the non-profit organization Skate Free, this facility – Miami's first public skate park – features two street courses, a competition-style bowl, a skate plaza and more. It is located underneath Interstate 95, so you'll hear the cars whizzing by overhead. Don't mind them. It's the wheels whizzing by next to you that you need to watch.

413 SOUNDSCAPE PARK / WALLCAST®

AT: NEW WORLD CENTER
500 17th St
South Beach ⑫
+1 305 673 3330
nws.edu

The domain of New World Center, home to New World Symphony, a world-class training orchestra, this green space is perfect for a picnic while you watch a concert or family-friendly movie outside on the high-tech WALLCAST®. Spread a blanket and bring some comfy sweaters. No one minds if little ones fall asleep.

414 PHILLIP AND PATRICIA FROST MUSEUM OF SCIENCE

AT: MUSEUM PARK
1101 Biscayne Blvd
Downtown ④
+1 305 434 9600
frostscience.org

Whether you're into the realm of outer space or the world under the sea, this is the place to observe exhibits, shows and programs. The Frost Planetarium is as high tech as NASA. The interactive, three-level Aquarium is simply one of a kind, re-creating the Gulf Stream, the Everglades and more.

415 GOLD COAST RAILROAD MUSEUM

12450 SW 152nd St
Deerwood ⑭
+1 305 253 0063
goldcoastrail
roadmuseum.org

Train buffs get a big kick out of this collection of 40+ real-world antique railcars, cabooses and locomotives. A couple of these are operational, so the museum offers rides most weekends, depending on crew and equipment availability. Other exhibits include model trains and Thomas the Tank play tables. Located next to Zoo Miami.

5

BIG ADVENTURES

416 THRILLER MIAMI SPEEDBOAT ADVENTURES

401 Biscayne Blvd
Downtown ④
+1 305 371 3278
thrillermiami.com

Few things are more exciting than speeding across the bay in a cigarette-style boat, leaving a huge wake in your, well, wake. This 45-minute ride takes you past the exclusive homes on Star and Fisher islands and also allows you to see South Beach. Not for the faint of heart – or stomach.

417 THE EDGE ROCK GYM

13972 SW 139th Court
West Kendall ⑭
+1 305 233 6623
theedgerockgym
miami.com

This 14.000-square-foot facility has been challenging climbers since 1998. Buy a discounted day pass with or without gear for the climb of your life. You can also take top rope belay classes, learn to lead climb and more. A counter on the website keeps track of how many climbers are in the gym so check before you go.

418 CORAL CASTLE MUSEUM

28655 S Dixie Hwy
Homestead ⑬
+1 305 248 6345
coralcastle.com

An engineering and architectural mystery, this structure and its 'furnishings' were carved entirely out of coral over the course of 28 years. No one can figure out how Ed Leedskalnin constructed items such as a 9-ton coral rock gate by himself – with homemade tools to boot. A fascinating stop on the way to the Keys.

419 DEZERLAND ACTION PARK MIAMI

14401 NE 19th Avenue North Miami ①
+1 786 590 5000
dezerlandpark.com/miami

With a trampoline park, go-karts, virtual reality, a ropes course, roller skating and more fun physically demanding activities, Dezerland is a go-to spot. Even better? It's all under one roof – literally. Everything is indoors, making this the perfect place to tire out the kids when it's raining or too hot outside.

420 BALLOON OVER MIAMI

20675 SW 162nd Ave Redland ⑬
+1 305 987 7788
balloonovermiami.com

Hot air ballooning is a unique and thrilling way to take in the beauty of the South Florida landscape and bask in its balmy weather. In fact, you can't actually fly when it's windy or rainy, so if you go up you're guaranteed calm tranquility. Cancellations or postponements may occur based on the weather. Otherwise, this 45-60-minute trip is a veritable sky safari.

418 CORAL CASTLE MUSEUM

20 PLACES
TO SLEEP

BOUTIQUE HOTELS

---

421 UMA HOUSE BY YURBAN SOUTH BEACH

1775 James Avenue
South Beach ⑫
+1 305 390 1184
umahouse
southbeach.com

If this hotel sounds like a song from Fiddler on the Roof, that's because they offer half of 136 rooms on the 'Sunrise' side of the building and the other half on the 'Sunset' side. Either way, you've got natural beauty on one end of the day. Plenty of little spaces in between include the courtyard and rooftop terraces, a pool and pool deck, and a beach lounge area complete with chairs and umbrellas.

422 GALE SOUTH BEACH

1690 Collins Avenue
South Beach ⑫
+1 305 673 0199
galehotel.com

An L. Murray Dixon-designed project from the 1940s, this renovation resulted in 87 chic, minimalist rooms that evoke vintage Capri. Perks include rainfall showers in the marble bathrooms, a rooftop pool and deck, and fabulous Italian food in Dolce Restaurant in the lobby.

423 KIMPTON SURFCOMBER HOTEL

1717 Collins Avenue
South Beach ⑫
+1 305 532 7715
www.surfcomber.com

Renovated in 2021, this posh boutique hotel has seen it all, from the time that South Beach was a coconut farm to the days it was Heaven's Waiting Room. Now the area is hip and trendy, and the Surfcomber is a chic, flower-laden haven where you can retreat from it all at the end of the evening. From personalized spa service to standout pet amenities, the hotel delivers a spot-on experience.

424 THE PLYMOUTH SOUTH BEACH

336 21st St
South Beach ⑬
+1 305 602 5000
theplymouth.com

This Anton Skislewicz-designed building was among the finest of its Streamline Moderne genre in 1940. The same is true now for the rooms that rim Collins Park or overlook the restored art deco pool. With inventive Blue Ribbon Sushi Bar & Grill on the premises, there's no need to leave.

425 EUROSTARS LANGFORD

121 SE 1st St
Downtown ④
+1 305 250 0782
eurostarshotels.co.uk/
eurostars-langford.html

One of the few boutique properties located in the heart of downtown, this Beaux Arts building – formerly Miami National Bank – combines august history from 1925 with today's high technology. Rooftop Bar Bloom Skybar features craft cocktails and attracts a Millennial-to-Gen X scene.

5 of the best
ROOMS WITH A VIEW

426 KIMPTON EPIC MIAMI

270 Biscayne
Boulevard Way
Downtown ④
+1 305 424 5226
epichotel.com

There's a reason why they call this a 'sky-rise boutique hotel.' And that's because of the 360-degree views of the Miami River, the Miami Circle, the downtown skyline and Biscayne Bay. Or maybe it's because of the scenic private balcony that you get. Or maybe it's because of the sights from up-high Area 31 or down-low at waterside Zuma.

427 CARILLON MIAMI WELLNESS RESORT

6801 Collins Avenue
North Beach ⑩
+1 866 800 3858
carillonhotel.com

Perched on the edge of North Beach, the Carillon offers a bastion of beautiful sights that are accompanied only by the sighing of ocean waves. Guests can soak in the views as they also practice the wellness routines they learn from on-staff experts.

428 MONDRIAN SOUTH BEACH

1100 West Avenue
South Beach ⑫
+1 305 514 1500
book.ennismore.com/
hotels/mondrian/
south-beach

Perched on the lip of land where the General Douglas MacArthur Causeway (I-395) kisses West Avenue, the Mondrian allows cosmic views of ocean and sky. Whether clear or stormy, it's always a performance out there, and every room at this dramatically designed hotel offers a front seat to it.

429 SAGAMORE SOUTH BEACH

1671 Collins Avenue
South Beach ⑫
+1 305 535 8088
sagamore
southbeach.com

Heavily involved with both the local and international visual arts scene, the Sagamore is known for its gallery-style design. But that doesn't mean that the views outside the rooms aren't just as stunning. Located right on the beach, the hotel's studios, queen rooms, and variety of suites all open up garden, pool, or South Beach views.

430 INTERCONTINENTAL MIAMI

100 Chopin Plaza
Downtown ④
+1 305 577 1000
icmiamihotel.com

The 34-story InterContinental pre-dates downtown Miami's renaissance. And while the stimulating views of Biscayne Bay have never changed, downtown now includes architecturally interesting arenas, museums, amphitheaters and parks. Even the hotel itself has LED artwork flashing on its side. No matter which direction you look, there's something exciting to see.

429 SAGAMORE SOUTH BEACH

The 5 most
LUXURIOUS HOTELS

---

431 FAENA HOTEL MIAMI BEACH

3201 Collins Avenue
Miami Beach ⑪
+1 305 534 8800
faena.com/miami-beach

This independent hotel is stunning in so many aspects it's difficult to list them all. Restaurants by globally-renowned chefs? Check. Design-rich bars and lounges that offer everything from private movie screenings to cabaret entertainment? Oh, yes. Important visual arts imported from Latin America? Indeed. It's a must-stay-to-be-believed kind of place.

432 THE SETAI MIAMI BEACH

2001 Collins Avenue
South Beach ⑫
+1 844 662 8387
thesetaihotel.com

Penultimate tranquility exists in this renovated Dempsey-Vanderbilt art deco building, initially designed by famed architect Henry Hohauser. Renowned for its customer service, The Setai never disappoints on any level. Both posh and zen from its rainfall showers and Frette linens to its exclusive spa treatments and culinary concoctions, it leads the beach in luxury.

433 THE MIAMI BEACH EDITION

2901 Collins Avenue
Miami Beach ⑩
+1 786 257 4500
marriott.com/en-us/
hotels/miaeb-the-
miami-beach-edition

The hotel to book when you have an appetite for all things luxury – fare from celebrity chef Jean-Georges Vongerichten; spectacular design; unparalleled spa treatments; and BASEMENT, a nightclub, bowling alley and ice-skating rink. During the day, nestle like a sea turtle on the private-access, 6503-square-meter beach or dive into the property's restored, original pool.

434 MR. C COCONUT GROVE

2988 McFarlane Road
Coconut Grove ⑧
+1 305 800 6672
mrchotels.com/
mrccoconutgrove

Run by brothers Ignazio and Maggio Cipriani, descendants of the inventor of the Bellini in Venice, this lovely Italian hotel offers 100 rooms and suites with private terraces and views of Biscayne Bay. Book a customized spa service, then cap it off with – naturally – a cocktail at the rooftop Bellini Miami restaurant.

435 NOBU HOTEL

AT: EDEN ROC
MIAMI BEACH
4525 Collins Avenue
Miami Beach ⑩
+1 305 704 7603
miamibeach.
nobuhotels.com

Designed by the Rockwell Group with high-end minimalism, this hotel-within-a-hotel offers a bespoke Japanese beach house experience. Guests have their own private adult-only pool, overlooking the Atlantic, away from other guests who stay at the larger Eden Roc property, as well as a Nobu Hotel section of the beach with a hospitality team. And, of course, Nobu Hotel guests can order the famous Nobu Restaurant cuisine from room service.

The 5 nicest
HOTEL POOLS

---

436 **THE BILTMORE**

1200 Anastasia Ave
Coral Gables ④
+1 305 445 1926
biltmorehotel.com

Renowned for its size – it was once the largest in the world – the Biltmore pool is 2137 square meters. It's also where the original Tarzan, actor Johnny Weissmüller, worked as a lifeguard. For the most luxe experience, rent a cabana and take an outdoor rain shower under native palms after a dip.

437 **THE STANDARD MIAMI BEACH**

40 Island Avenue
South Beach ⑬
+1 305 673 1717
*standardhotels.com/
miami/properties/
miami-beach*

Complete with a hydrotherapy spa with plenty of outdoor soaking tubs of different styles and temperatures, this hotel perches like a heron on the Venetian Causeway. As does the main zero-entry pool, which would look like it continues straight into the bay if it weren't for the bright yellow lounge chairs on the deck.

438 **NATIONAL HOTEL MIAMI BEACH**

1677 Collins Avenue
South Beach ⑫
+1 305 532 2311
nationalhotel.com

This pair of pools – one more of a square, the other a thin rectangle – includes the longest infinity-edge pool in Miami Beach. Fringed by palm trees and other assorted native foliage that provides shade, the pools are so tempting you might never make it to the beach. *C'est la vida loca.*

439 1 HOTEL SOUTH BEACH

2341 Collins Avenue
South Beach ⑬
+1 866 615 1111
1hotels.com/south-beach

Deeply concerned with sustainability, 1 Hotel incorporates design with ecologically sound practices. This ethos extends to the South Pool, the Center Pool, the adult-only Rooftop Pool and the private Cabana Pool, where the day beds and cabanas utilize reclaimed wood and natural fabrics and all views of the ocean are pristine and panoramic.

440 FOUR SEASONS HOTEL AT THE SURF CLUB

9011 Collins Avenue
Surfside ⑭
+1 305 381 3333
fourseasons.com/
surfside

This is not just any Four Seasons, and this is not just any pool. The renovated Surf Club was home to Harvey Firestone and his Rat Pack friends. The beachside pool is just an extension of this elegant palazzo. You almost expect a serenade as you lounge by the palm trees.

436 THE BILTMORE

BISCAYNE NATIONAL PARK

50 WEEKEND ACTIVITIES

5 *intimate*
WELLNESS FACILITIES

---

441 BREATHE PILATES MIAMI

8650 Biscayne Boulevard, #31 El Portal ①
+1 786 275 4128
breathepilates miami.com

This lovely, full-service Pilates studio offers classes and private lessons. But even the classes can feel like individual sessions due to the size of them – they're restricted to the five reformers available. Talented instructors, headed by owner Gretchen Wagoner, and engaging specials also tempt the typical studio jumper to stay put.

442 TANTRA STUDIOS

390 NE 59th Terrace MiMo District/ Upper East Side ②
+1 305 992 0754
tantra-studios.com

You never know what wellness event this holistic space might be hosting – a yoga retreat, a spirit dance, a vinyasa flow and sound bath, a kundalini activation process or a transformation through movement, breath and sound. Some events, though, like Tantra Mondays, repeat weekly. Whatever you choose to do here, you'll feel soothed by the low-key vibe and re-energized by the interaction with the knowledgeable guides.

443 THE SACRED SPACE

105 NE 24th St
Wynwood ③
sacredspacemiami.com

Too often, wellness can feel trendy. That's never the case at The Sacred Space, where being and feeling complete and healthy – and treating the earth as the same – has always been a calling. Take classes in yoga, meditation, or sound work, or do something out of your wellness comfort zone and try regenerative farming, cacao ceremonies, and biohacking technology.

444 FEEL THE HEAL

717 NE 79th St
MiMo District/
Upper East Side ②
+1 305 466 9268
feeltheheal.com

Traveling can be tough on the digestive system. So can daily stress. Visit this studio to detox the body through colonic irrigation, abdominal cupping, ear candling and more. Looking for foot ion or liver gallbladder detox? Heal here. Or simply get in bathing suit shape with a cellulite body or mud wrap.

445 BODYSENSE

2292 Coral Way
Coral Gables ⑧
+1 305 854 3100
bodysenseusa.com

Feel better through medical, postpartum, sports and Oriental foot massages, among other types. Balance your skin and rid it of impurities by way of various facials, including de-reddening and anti-aging. You can even get screened for early breast cancer here through thermography. Whether the wellness is mental or physical, BodySense has you covered.

The 5 best small
SPAS and SALONS

─────────

446 GG SALON & SPA

9063 Biscayne Blvd
Miami Shores ①
+1 305 759 9710
ggsalonspa.com

A full-service establishment for the
whole family, this salon is run like
a family institution. In fact, it is a family
institution. Now owned by second-
generation GG – daughter Gloriane –
the salon's services range from classic to
trendy. And you can still book first-gen
GG as an eyebrow specialist. As always,
products are organic and wellness-
oriented. Book online for convenience.

447 BELLEZZA

5734 Sunset Drive
South Miami ⑨
+1 305 284 0669
bellezzaspa.com

The combination of salon services, spa
offerings and med-spa features turn this
establishment into an all-day experience.
Combine a facial or microdermabrasion
with a body scrub and massage, and
follow it up with beautifying hair and nail
treatments. A dedicated staff diagnoses
your skin/hair type before you begin.

448 SKIN BY TATUM

1819 West Ave, Unit 1
South Beach ⑫
+1 305 531 5994
skinbytatum.com

Founder Tatum Fritts, who has a lot of education and experience in the skin field, can make you glow. Put yourself in those knowledgeable hands and let them exfoliate, detox, steam, scrub and more. You'll leave with visible results, and some knowledge of your own on how to maintain that radiant exterior.

449 BEAUTY SHOP MIAMI

8361 NE 2nd Avenue
Little River ②
+1 305 603 7253
beautyshopmiami.com

Aptly named for the way cofounders and life partners Drew Calloway and Martin Ducasse make you feel, Beauty Shop offers an array of hair services. This swanky, affable shop operates in a very slowly gentrifying strip mall but pay no mind: The glam is inside. And it's also inside you as soon as they get their hands on your head.

450 SANA SKIN STUDIO

167 NW 25th St
Wynwood ③
+1 305 707 5176
sanaskinstudio.com

You don't expect to find this great little boutique on a crowded, perpetually-under-construction side street in busy, party-happy Wynwood. But there it is, the answer to all your skin's needs and dreams. No matter your age and skin type, there's a facialist and a product for you, along with a lot of help in lifting, smoothing, firming, detoxifying and reducing discoloration, fine lines acne and more.

5 things to do in
BISCAYNE NATIONAL PARK

9700 SW 328th St
Homestead ⑬
+1 305 230 1114 X555
nps.gov/bisc

451 **DIVE AND SNORKEL THE MARITIME HERITAGE TRAIL**

SCUBA divers and snorkeling buffs get more than their fill exploring 100 years worth of underwater wrecks. Comprising six ships that date back to 1878, the sites can only be reached by boat. The Fowey Rocks Lighthouse, which was supposed to prevent the ships from grounding on the reefs, is also part of the trail.

452 **KAYAK AND CANOE TO THE BOCA CHITA KEY LIGHTHOUSE**

Biscayne Bay is so shallow in spots it's almost like you're paddling in a giant puddle. Don't be fooled. The over 11-kilometer distance to Boca Chita Key to climb the lighthouse, built in the 1930s, is a shoulder-stretching one. Rent at Dante Fascell Visitor Center Wednesday-Sunday or bring your own and launch for free.

453 FISH OVER CORAL REEFS

The living coral reefs provide a vast array of species for both sport and dining purposes. But the reefs also pose boating challenges, and the convoluted laws – the park is federal, but fishing and harvesting is taken care of by the state – create others. Check seasons, prohibitions, and licensing regulations before you begin.

454 VISIT THE MUSEUM AT CONVOY POINT

The park, 95 percent of which is underwater, actually has four different ecosystems. Learn about them at the museum through multi-media exhibits. Kids can touch everything from bones and feathers to sponges and coral, and adults can admire displays of local art inspired by the park.

455 CAMP AT ELLIOTT KEY

The park's largest island has facilities including grills and rest rooms with cold running water. You can make the 27,4-kilometer round trip in a canoe or take the boat that leaves the Visitor Center daily at 8 am and Elliott Key at 9 am. The campsite costs 35 dollars; transportation fees are separate.

5 lovely
DAY TRIPS

---

456 KEY LARGO

KEY LARGO
VISITOR CENTER
106000 Overseas Hwy,
Mile Marker 106
Key Largo
The Keys ⑬
+1 305 451 1414
keylargochamber.org

This large island is home to the historic Key Largo Rock Castle or the century-old African Queen, used on the 1951 movie. Spot wildlife at John Pennekamp State Park, the Florida Keys Wild Bird Center or the Florida Keys National Marine Sanctuary. And swim with everyone's favorite marine mammals at Oceanside Dolphins.

457 LAS OLAS BOULEVARD

Fort Lauderdale
lasolasboulevard.com

Pleasantly panoramic, the heart of Fort Lauderdale's downtown district is filled with artsy shops, fashionable boutiques and trendy indoor/outdoor cafes and bars. It's slightly more relaxed than Miami's main thoroughfares, but no less fabulous for people watching. Las Olas also hosts annual festivals and art shows.

456 KEY LARGO

457 LAS OLAS BOULEVARD

458 ISLAMORADA

ISLAMORADA
VISITORS CENTER
87100 Overseas Hwy,
Mile Marker 87
Islamorada
The Keys ⑬
+1 305 664 4503
islamorada
chamber.com

Islamorada is famous for the Tiki Bar at Postcard Inn Beach Resort & Marina at Holiday Isle; Green Turtle Inn; and Islamorada Fish Company. If you don't feel like drinking or eating, browse the Rain Barrel Artisan's Village – and greet the humongous lobster named Betsy out front. Great photo opp.

459 ROSEMARY SQUARE

S Rosemary Avenue
Downtown
West Palm Beach
+1 561 366 1000
thesquarewestpalm.com

This chic and trendy downtown region in West Palm Beach features high-end farm-to-table restaurants, boutiques filled with fashion and galleries where artisans exhibit their wares. Take cooking classes at Sur La Table, enjoy family events like Bubble Blast, splash in the *Water Pavilion West Palm* and check out the public art including *The Wishing Tree,* whose 10.000 leaves are embedded with 100.000 programmable LED lights. Only an hour from Miami using the high-speed rail Brightline from MiamiCentral Station.

460 ROB'S REDLAND RIOT SELF-GUIDED TOUR

Redland/Homestead
redlandriot.com

Get in your car and follow the directives to a dozen spots in the Redland/Homestead farming region. These include Knaus Berry Farm for incredible cinnamon rolls; Schnebly Redland's Winery & Brewery, where fermentation begins with tropical fruits; and Cauley Square, a historic village of antique shops with a quaint tearoom.

5 waterways and marinas for
WATERSPORTS and
FISHING charters

461 **OLETA RIVER STATE PARK**

3400 NE 163rd St
North Miami Beach ①
+1 305 919 1846
*floridastateparks.org/
OletaRiver*

Located in the middle of the city, Oleta is known for its outstanding water access. Swim from the 366-meter beach; fish the Intracoastal Waterway; or stand-up paddleboard, kayak or canoe through Oleta River into Biscayne Bay. To book paddling and kayak tours, go to *oletariveroutdoors.com.*

462 **VENETIAN MARINA & YACHT CLUB**

1635 N Bayshore Dr
Downtown ④
+1 786 785 1679
*integramarinas.com/
venetian-marina*

Host to the Miami International Boat Show, an extravaganza of deep-water showing off, this marina offers 186 slips right next to Kaseya Center. Charter a happy hour cruise or a day of fishing at this full-service marina filled with amenities, then disembark in the thick of Downtown and the Brickell Financial District. Watch the speedboats and yachts cruise east to the bay, west through the Miami River, or back to their slips, depending on the time of day.

463 MIAMI BEACH MARINA

300 Alton Road
South Beach ⑫
+1 305 673 6000
miamibeach
marina.com

South Beach's 400-plus-slip marina provides plenty of services ranging from picnic provisions at Marine Deii to sightseeing tours at Ocean Force Adventures. For SCUBA and snorkeling gear, head into Tarpoon Lagoon Diving Center. To go parasailing, book FlySOBE Parasail. You can pretty much get all you need here, from a new golf cart to concert tickets. Grab a happy hour drink at Monty's and hop a ride on the Water taxi to your next location.

464 DINNER KEY MARINA & MOORING FACILITY

3400 Pan American Dr
Coconut Grove ⑧
+1 305 329 4755
miami.gov/Parks-
Public-Places/Marinas

The historic home for Pan American Airways 'flying boats', this marina is renowned for sailing lessons and charters. Novices and seasoned sailors alike can appreciate the breadth of instruction and boat selection – and so can those who prefer to just sit back, let others do the tacking and be taken on a tour.

465 BILL BIRD MARINA

10800 Collins Avenue
Sunny Isles Beach ①
+1 305 947 3525
www.miamidade.gov/
parks/bill-bird.asp

Because the marina is sandwiched between the ocean and the Intracoastal, a large fleet of sport and drift fishing boats camps out here, waiting for avid clients who don't like to go very far before dropping a line. A dive boat, boat and Jet Ski rentals and plenty of other amenities are on hand, too.

The 5 most beautiful
BIKE RIDES

---

466 SHARK VALLEY
VISITORS CENTER
AT: EVERGLADES NP
36000 SW 8th St
Miami ⑬
+1 305 221 8776
nps.gov/ever/
planyourvisit/
svdirections.htm

Pedal around alligators (not sharks) on this 24-kilometer path in Everglades National Park. A variety of the reptiles are usually sunning themselves on the pavement. Don't worry – they're somnolent and not going to chase you as you ride by. Also look for dozens of subtropical bird, amphibian and mammal species while you ride. Rentals available.

467 RICKENBACKER
TRAIL
Rickenbacker Cwy
Key Biscayne ⑥
traillink.com/trail/
rickenbacker-trail

From the toll through the islands of Virginia Key and Key Biscayne, as well as along the beaches. This causeway is the equivalent to a mountain in Miami, and the only elevation where serious cyclists can train. It also happens to be gorgeous, with water sparkling and beaches gleaming on both sides. Do take care to watch traffic, as drivers are not always watching you.

466 SHARK VALLEY

468 SNAKE CREEK TRAIL

North Miami Beach ①
miamidade.gov/
parksmasterplan/
library/snake.pdf

From Florida's Turnpike in Miami Gardens to NE 19th Avenue in North Miami Beach. Paved and perfectly flat, this 10,5-kilometer path is a pleasant bike ride for the entire family. It twists and turns by a canal enhanced with fitness stations and shade shelters. Park at Barry Schreiber Promenade (NE 172nd St and S Glades Drive) or Snake Creek Linear Park (NE 169th St and NE 15th Avenue).

469 OLD CUTLER TRAIL

Old Cutler Rd
and SW 224th St
in Cutler Bay to
Old Cutler Rd and
Cocoplum Circle
in Coral Gables
www.miamidade.gov/
parksmasterplan/
library/OCT.pdf

This stunning, 17,7-kilometer ride takes you through Miami's southern neighborhoods and under the canopies of old ficus and banyan trees. Stops along the route for botany lovers might include Matheson Hammock Park, Fairchild Tropical Botanic Garden and Pinecrest Gardens. Riders should be a little experienced, as the tree roots stipple sidewalks and streets.

470 VIRGINIA KEY NORTH POINT TRAILS

AT: VIRGINIA KEY
MOUNTAIN BIKE PARK
Arthur Lamb Jr Road
Virginia Key ⑥
virginiakey
bicycleclub.org

Dedicated mountain bikers will be thrilled to know that even at sea level, you can train on some pretty tough terrain. The 7,5 miles of trails were built and are maintained by private donors, so if you go to enjoy them, consider donating afterward. And do check out the site map before you ride.

The 5 greatest
GOLF COURSES

471 MIAMI SHORES COUNTRY CLUB

10000 Biscayne Blvd
Miami Shores ①
+1 305 795 2360
miamishoresgolf.com

This 18-hole, country club golf course has both history and reasonable prices going for it. In addition to some gorgeous, subtropical landscaping, there's plenty of wildlife, including an albino fox and Florida coyotes that live here. Non-resident tee times are listed on the site.

472 JW MARRIOTT MIAMI TURNBERRY RESORT & SPA

19999 W Country
Club Drive
Aventura ①
+1 305 932 6200
marriott.com

Where else can you play with pink flamingos? They gather, along with swans and ducks, at the water features on these two famed 18-hole courses, originally designed by Robert Trent Jones Sr., then redesigned by Raymond Floyd. They're home to PGA and LPGA tournaments – but also where fledglings can learn to fly.

473 MIAMI BEACH GOLF CLUB

2301 Alton Road
South Beach ⑪⑫
+1 305 532 3350
miamibeach
golfclub.com

These lovingly groomed greens were once known as the neglected Bayshore Golf Course, built in 1923. Now thriving with a Jim McLean Golf Academy on the premises, it truly fulfills original developer Carl Fisher's dream for it. The club embraces visitors of all ages and also allows installations during Art Basel.

474 CRANDON GOLF AT KEY BISCAYNE

**6700 Crandon Blvd
Key Biscayne ⑥
+1 305 361 9129**
golfcrandon.com

With a stunning backdrop of downtown Miami and a foreground of Biscayne Bay, Crandon practically begs visitors to play golf, if only for the views. Its beautifully kept public course is also one of the hardest par-72 in the state. That seventh hole… well, there's a reason it makes *Golf Digest*. Pros play here.

475 GRANADA GOLF COURSE

**2001 Granada Blvd
Coral Gables ⑨
+1 305 460 5367**
coralgables.com

When you don't have much time, try this 9-hole, par-36 course. Debuting in 1923, it's the oldest of its kind in the state. Perfect for beginners or more seasoned golfers who want to get in a few rounds, followed by a meal at the 10th hole, aka Burger Bob's.

472 JW MARRIOTT MIAMI TURNBERRY RESORT & SPA

5 terrific **TENNIS** and **PICKLEBALL** facilities

476 CRANDON PARK TENNIS CENTER
7300 Crandon Blvd
Key Biscayne ⑥
+1 305 365 2300
www.miamidade.gov/parks/crandon-tennis.asp

Hard courts? Yes. Clay? Certainly. Grass? You betcha. That's because these 26 courts, half of which are lighted, are not only for residents and visitors to utilize. The Miami Open used to be played here. Now it sponsors The Crandon Cup as well as 14 USTA junior and two USTA adult tournaments. Lessons, classes, camps and more.

477 SIP AND PICKLE
AT: WYNWOOD MARKETPLACE
2250 NW 2nd Avenue
Wynwood ③
sipandpickle.com

You knew it was inevitable, right? So you might as well take advantage of the fact that you can now pickle yourself inside and out. Purchase one-hour packages online which include premium beer or wine, waters, Red Bulls, and equipment for four. Just remember: After you've had a drink or two, no ball is worth going the distance for.

478 PENNY SUGARMAN TENNIS CENTER AT SANS SOUCI

1795 Sans Souci Blvd
North Miami ①
+1 305 893 7130
northmiamifl.gov/
facilities/facility/
details/Penny-Sugar
man-Tennis-Center-
at-Sans-Sou-30

Hidden on a side street behind a convenience store, this tennis center has more ambition than it appears. Professional trainers, spring and summer camps, and opportunities for USTA junior memberships and teams abound. All ages, including 'tiny tots', are encouraged to play on the 13 lighted (12 clay and 1 hard) courts.

479 RIVIERA TENNIS CENTER

9775 SW 87th Avenue
Kendall ⑭
+1 305 775 4727
rivieratenniscenter.com

If pickleball sounds intimidating to those new to the sport or longtime tennis players, head to Riviera. Here, they offer professionals, lessons, gear, outfits, and courts for those who want to learn the newest, trendiest sport. And for those who don't? They still have dedicated tennis courts so you can play what you've always enjoyed.

480 FLAMINGO PARK TENNIS CENTER

1200 Meridian Ave
South Beach ⑬
+1 305 673 7761
flamingotennis
center.com

Strategy and fitness clinics and camps for both adults and kids. Events like Guys' or Girls' Night Out. Competitive and social tournaments organized for locals. Retreats designed for corporations. At these clay courts, tennis is a community sport as well as a way to meet new friends. Note: One non-dedicated pickleball court is located at the handball court; first come, first serve.

5 fun places to
PLAY or WATCH
SOCCER

481 URBAN INDOOR FUTBOL

1125 NW 71st St
West Little River ②
+1 786 253 2888
urbanindoorfutbol.com

Formerly Urban Soccer Five in Wynwood, this business is now six indoor, smal turf fields in West Little River. Play 5v5 or 6v6 games or tournaments, or try the first hard-floor futsal court in Miami (where you can also play basketball). A bar shows pro games on a wide screen.

482 PEGASO SOCCER

177 NE 21st St
Edgewater ③
+1 786 292 3404
pegasosoccer.com

Open 6 am to nearly 3 am and booked by the hour, these three different size fields allow you to play 5x5, 6x6, 7x7. The versatility is ideal for when you can only get a pickup game going with a certain amount of players due to illness or injury. Don't have a gang or regulars or a team to play with? Connect to other athletes looking for a game via the pickup play *plei.app* and join a game at Pegaso (or elsewhere).

483 INDOOR SOCCER PRO

1128 NW 159th Drive
Miami Gardens ①
+1 305 454 0900
indoorsoccerpro.com

Open from 8 am to midnight, this air-conditioned futsal/indoor soccer facility offers the usual youth development training, leagues and tournaments on its three 5v5 fields. As additional features, it provides 'soccer-sitting' – a place to leave your kids for some activity on days off from school and when you need a night out.

484 REVO BY ARENA MADNESS

10395 NW 41st St, #101
Doral ⑯
+1 305 717 0020
revosoccer.com

Revo claims to have the biggest indoor 6v6 fields and the best, FIFA-approved artificial grass in the city. It also offers a functional training gym for adults and serves as an Arena Strikers Academy for kids. On a less serious – or maybe more serious? – note: it also offers a fully outfitted sports bar with a cinema screen where you can indulge your passion for your pro team.

485 SOCCER ROOFTOP MIAMI

444 Brickell Avenue, 2nd Floor
Brickell ⑤
+1 305 967 3512
soccerrooftop miami.com

The game doesn't get any better than when it's played on pro-style turf on the top of a building in downtown Miami. Lighted, netted and padded courts make sure that no one hurls themselves into – or off – something dangerous, and lounges, locker rooms and concessions add to the overall futbol vibe. Book by the hour for whatever event – practice, game, or party – you desire.

485 SOCCER ROOFTOP MIAMI

5 *fascinating places to*
WATCH OR LEARN LATIN DANCE

---

486 SALSA ART STUDIOS

1501 SW 8th St
Little Havana ⑦
+1 786 487 1992
salsa-art.com

Before heading out to Miami's super fun Latin nightclubs, figure out the steps. In other words, learn how to move your hips. And you don't have to embarrass yourself by taking a group class. This dance school, located in the heart of Little Havana, provides private lessons. Ask for Jumaqui when you call.

487 CALLE DRAGONES

1036 SW 8th St
Little Havana ⑦
*calledragones.com/
home-english*

A tribute to Havana's Chinatown, which harkens back to the 1850s. It also includes some more modern references to Studio 54, Moulin Rouge, and Cirque du Soleil. Regardless, this exciting dinner theater is about both the show and the food, courtesy of the talented troupe and award-winning Cuban chef and cookbook Louis Pous. Reservations highly recommended.

488 MOJITOS CALLE 8

8000 SW 8th St
Westchester ⑭
+1 305 406 1002

If you're shy, wait until the nightly cabaret show before hitting the dance floor. Otherwise, watch the locals, who dance between courses of delicious Cuban food all washed down with that minty, rummy drink for which the place is named. Once you get the hang of it, you'll never want to stop.

489 MANGO'S TROPICAL CAFÉ

900 Ocean Drive
South Beach ⑫
+1 305 673 4422
salsamia.com/miami-
salsa-classes
mangos.com

Mango's is known for its risqué sidewalk shows. But what some don't know is that you can purchase salsa and bachata lessons, along with a table for your party from 7-10 pm, a mojito, and a three-appetizer tasting. After your tutorial, stay until 5 am, practice your skills, and access to the service to assuage your thirst and hunger pangs.

490 CLUB TÍPICO DOMINICANO

1344 NW 36th St
Allapattah ③
+1 305 634 7819
clubtipico
dominicano.com

It may seem like otherwise sometimes, but Miami is filled with Latin cultures outside of Cuba. Check out a slice of Dominican life at this long-running restaurant and nightclub, where there's always a DJ or artist performing and guests getting up to dance. Join in or order another drink and watch; either way, it's the spirit of Miami that moves you.

10 RANDOM FACTS
ABOUT MIAMI

---

5 sites to visit
WHERE FAMOUS SCENES WERE FILMED

491 JIMMY'S EASTSIDE DINER

7201 Biscayne Blvd
MiMo District/
Upper East Side ②
+1 305 754 3692

This long-running diner, open for breakfast and lunch only, appears in the Academy Award-winning film *Moonlight*, set in Miami. The mahogany-colored booths and checkered curtains are the perfect set for the emotional scene, during which the lead reunites with an influential figure from his past.

492 BIG PINK

157 Collins Avenue
South Beach ⑫
+1 305 532 4700
*mylesrestaurant
group.com/big-pink*

Open until late night, this retro diner was originally a collaboration between Michael Schwartz (Michael's Genuine) and Myles Chefetz (Prime 112), today two of the most successful restaurateurs in the city. In the Farrelly Brothers comedy *There's Something About Mary*, it was featured as meeting location for two characters.

493 THE CARLYLE

1250 Ocean Drive
South Beach ⑫
*southbeach
rentalsonline.com*

Among the first art deco hotels to be resurrected on Ocean Drive (and now a residential building), The Carlyle Hotel, built in 1939, is symbolic of South Beach. Some of the largest productions filmed there, before and after renovation, include *Scarface*, *The Birdcage* and *Bad Boys II*.

494 LESLIE HOTEL

1244 Ocean Drive
South Beach ⑫
+1 786 476 2645
lesliehotel.com

Watching the 1994 comedy *Ace Ventura: Pet Detective* is an architectural history lesson. Because the movie was filmed largely on South Beach, you can spot many art deco masterpieces in their before or after stages of redevelopment. The Leslie, constructed in 1937, is one of the most recognizable.

495 SOUTH MIAMI AVENUE BASCULE BRIDGE

400 N Miami Avenue
Downtown ④
+1 305 374 3829
marinas.com/view/
bridge/4ju43_South_
Miami_Avenue_
Bascule_Bridge_FL_
United_States

Built in 1985 and improved in 2015 – now it's bicycle-friendly! – this drawbridge has been useful. Sure, boats of all types can continue along the Miami River. But film directors who need to map out car races and chases in productions like *2 Fast, 2 Furious* and *Miami Vice* have also cashed in.

493 THE CARLYLE

494 LESLIE HOTEL

5
NEED-TO-KNOW FACTS
about Miami

---

496 **DRESS CODES**

Because it's very hot in Miami for six months, women sometimes seem to dress in as little as possible, and men do not don dinner jackets even in formal restaurants. That said, the air conditioning in public places can make it chilly. And being shirtless or in bathing suits inside is bad form.

497 **RULES OF THE ROAD**

Miami's roadways are limited with too-few main arteries and near-constant construction. The beaches are connected to the mainland by causeways with drawbridges, creating more traffic. Drivers come from many different countries and don't always obey local laws. Drive defensively and always use a current app or Sat-Nav system.

498 PUBLIC TRANSPORTATION AND PARKING

miamigov.com,
miamibeachfl.gov,
coralgables.com,
cityofdoral.com,
www.miamidade.gov/
global/transportation/
home.page

The Metrobus, Metrorail and Metromover are helpful for moving around on the mainland, especially Brickell/Downtown. Municipalities have their own trolley systems, which is useful in places like South Beach, where parking is tight. Check your car in at beautifully designed garages like the Herzog & de Meuron project on Lincoln Road, then trolley to various destinations.

499 TIPPING POLICIES

Err on the generous side. Leave 18-20 percent tip for food/drink service and spa treatments. But always check your bill – some establishments add it automatically. Tip valets 5 dollars when your car is returned. Bellhops receive 5 dollars per bag; door attendants who unload your car or hail taxis, 5 dollars. For housekeeping, 5 to 10 dollars per night.

500 LAWS AND MANDATES

You will see people flaunting liquor and drug laws in places like Wynwood and South Beach, which may lead to imitation. Be clear: open containers of liquor are not allowed in public outside of bars and restaurants, and marijuana in any form is only legal if you are licensed for a medical marijuana card. Masks for COVID-19 are not required anywhere in Florida; however, you're welcome to wear one if it makes you feel comfortable. Some establishments will require their employees to mask but they can't require the same of guests.

INDEX

COLOPHON

EDITING *and* COMPOSING – Jen Karetnick

GRAPHIC DESIGN – Joke Gossé and doublebill.design

PHOTOGRAPHY – Valerie Sands – vsandsphotography.com

ADDITIONAL PHOTOGRAPHY – p. 37: Julia Rose Photography –
p. 60, 93: World Red Eye – p. 69: Joia Beach – p. 95: Rosa Sky Rooftop –
p. 113: InterContinental Miami – p. 114, 123: Bethania Canavesi –
p. 118: CocoWalk – p. 136: Miami Nautique International

COVER IMAGE – Leslie Hotel (secret 494)

The addresses in this book have been selected after thorough independent
research by the author, in collaboration with Luster Publishing. The selection
is solely based on personal evaluation of the business by the author. Nothing
in this book was published in exchange for payment or benefits of any kind.

D/2022/12.005/24
ISBN 978 94 6058 3308
NUR 513, 510

© 2017 Luster Publishing, Antwerp
FOURTH REVISED EDITION, MAY 2024 – Third reprint, May 2024
lusterpublishing.com – THE500HIDDENSECRETS.COM
info@lusterpublishing.com

Printed in Italy by Printer Trento.

MIX
Paper | Supporting
responsible forestry
FSC® C015829